STOP DOUBTING, START LEADING: YOUR OWN UNIQUE WAY

BY LEONIE GREEN

First published in 2019 by Corvus Group Australia, 14/23A Cook Road Mitcham

© Leonie T Green 2019

Book design: Ckaos

Printed: Ingram Spark, Australia

Disclaimer:
The material throughout this publication is only representative of general comments, instead of professional advice. Its intention is not to provide specific guidance for any particular circumstances. It should not be relied upon for any decision to take action or not to take action on any matter which it covers. Readers should obtain professional advice wherever appropriate, and before making any such decision. To the maximum extent permitted by law, the author and publisher disclaim all responsibility and liability to any person, arising directly or indirectly from any person taking or not taking action based on the information in this book.

Contents

Why me, why now?

S o you are a leader? Well done. This is great, we need more of them in the world. So what is that voice of doubt in your head?

You've been promoted to a leadership role because someone saw *you*. They saw what was possible; they saw what you were capable of doing today and tomorrow. You might not see that yet, but they did.

Let's make sure that the voice of doubt (that others can't hear) doesn't get in the way of your ability to lead with your own personal flair.

Crises of Confidence are inevitable

Confidence is critical to all leaders. And yet, *all* leaders have moments of crisis when it comes to confidence. All leaders have, at some point in time, let the doubting voice triumph.

We all have moments of doubt. What matters most is what we do about it. We want to make sure that, upon the crisis of confidence occurring, we are ready to act decisively and still lead through it.

Communication, comparison and competence: they're within your control

What I know for sure is that confidence is a combination of elements which are within our control if we understand them and take action. This book is about breaking down those key elements: communication, comparison and competence. The book also provides easy, practical steps which you can take immediately. All these steps will improve how you work with yourself.

As leaders, we all need to be able to lead ourselves. We need to be able to say, "Oh hell yeah, I want to work with you. You're great." Can you say that to yourself right now? And, if not, then this might be why you picked up this book. By the end of the book, I'd like to think that the above-mentioned sentence becomes an easier one for you to say to yourself.

Can you relate?!

Imagine going to work each morning thinking, "Ugh, I need to work with this brain and body today. It never works for me and it's not making me feel very vibrant. I'm not looking forward to it at all." Ever had one of those days? Had many of those days in a row?

If that's your type of self-talk, you will not be getting the best from your brain and body. Imagine instead that you head to work in the morning while saying, "Today I'm going to learn something new. I'm going to be my own greatest supporter. And, I'm going to work on improving my current personal best."

Imagine the difference it could now have on your day.

I'm talking from experience

This book has come from my own experience. It also comes from my experience of working with executive managers and leaders. I have seen consistent experiences and consistent stories. I have seen so many new and experienced leaders who really struggle to get past doubt.

It will impact your performance if you are stuck in doubt the majority of the time. This book is about giving you tools to counter the voice of doubt while starting to build an alternative voice.

I have seen executives who burned out quickly because they believed the voice of doubt. I was one of them (more on that later). I don't want that for you.

I started my career as a lawyer working with employers, advising them on employment law. I love employment law. I love the law's ability to influence the relationship of employee and employer. At the same time, I wanted to better understand the other factors that influence the relationship of employer and employee (or leader and team member) beyond compliance with the law. So, I joined the corporate world after leaving my work as an employment lawyer.

I worked in industrial relations, shared services (payroll, credit, customer care), and then human resources.

My early corporate roles were still about compliance. Compliance with the law mostly. But, what I enjoyed the most (and found myself doing with each new team) was building capability in people and teams. I left the corporate world in early 2014 to set up my own business. I wanted to do more on building capability. Particularly building the capability of leaders.

Leadership capability within organisations is critical. That's where you get the uplift or your corporate edge. It's leadership that can result in people giving their discretionary effort, rather than just doing their job (at best) or shirking all responsibility (at worst). Leadership is all about getting the best out of your people; however, in order to do get the best out of someone else, you've got to get the best out of yourself. You've got to do the work on yourself. You've got to be able to lead yourself well. And, if you can't lead yourself well, then you are going to struggle to lead anybody else.

Let's get started...

This book focuses on understanding confidence through communication, comparison, and competence.

Self-leadership leads to self-confidence. And, it's the first step towards leading others.

I see leaders who falter because they're not focusing on themselves – they're focusing on everyone else. Remember the advice you get during the safety demonstration before a flight? Put your own mask on first.

It's time to do the work on yourself.

But first, let's continue onto chapter one so that we may discover the first step. Let's talk about how we communicate with ourselves.

1 Communication: How the stories you tell yourself make (or break) you

A S A HUMAN BEING, you are wired to communicate in one way or another. You talk, wink, smile, yell, argue, or laugh. This is the world of communication which occurs with others. It's the outer world of communication.

When it comes to confidence, the world of communication that makes the biggest difference is the communication you have with yourself – the inner world of communication. The stories you tell yourself. The stories to which you listen – sometimes without realising it.

Stories we tell ourselves sometimes feel like advertisements for movies which we never want to see again; yet, we can't seem to turn them off. They play in our mind's eye with all their vibrancy, trying to remind us of something while often trying to scare us into taking action or running away.

I love the way *The Holiday*, a romantic comedy, highlights this. Throughout this Christmas family favourite, Amanda Woods is a movie trailer producer (movie preview producer if you live in Australia). As a self-proclaimed workaholic, it's only natural that she thinks in movie previews! As she heads off on a holiday escape, we see one of her 'movie preview thoughts.'

'Amanda Woods is proud to present...her life. She had it all: The job. The house. The guy. This holiday season, find out what Amanda doesn't have.'

We then see Amanda's reaction to her thoughts: an *arrgh* and a cringe; and, that get-me-out-of-here look.

I have this same look when one of my movie preview stories plays. I don't have a great poker face. I am sure people see the look (often a cringe or a severe frown) when one of those stories flashes across my brain. I know my body language gives it away as I catch myself in it. I am either slumped or my shoulders are tensed up around my ears – or both!

Consider when you last replayed a movie preview to yourself. Was it a story that highlighted how amazing you are? Or, was it a story that pulled you down? The stories we tend to repeat are the ones highlighting what is *not*, rather than what could be or even what really is.

We can catch ourselves doing it, but often we are already in the downward spiral when we do. That can result in us getting stuck. Stuck as in 'I suck.'

The 'I suck' stories

I love kids' movies. I learn from them all the time. Often I am laughing and crying alongside my daughter as we learn (and re-learn) the salient life lessons that children's movies contain. *Kung Fu Panda* is a favourite, and one of my favourite characters is Po Ping. In part, the concept of 'I suck' stories was inspired by Po.

In Kung Fu Panda, Master Oogway announces, *'The universe has brought us the dragon warrior.'* Standing before him is Po Ping, the most unlikely of dragon warriors. The dragon warrior is supposed to be a prodigy and the one who will unlock the secret to the dragon scroll. The famous Kung Fu Furious Five assume it will be one of them, most likely Tigress. But instead, Master Oogway points directly to Po – cuddly, rotund, loveable, food-loving and kind-hearted Po Ping. Po was not convinced that Master Oogway had made the right call. Po knew he loved Kung Fu, but still felt inadequate. Indeed most of those around him tended to believe his version of inadequacy. All except Master Oogway.

After an arduous (and fairly embarrassing) day of training, and after over-hearing the Kung Fu Furious Five making fun of him, Po escapes. He tries to block out his feelings with food. On this occasion, he accidentally stuffs his face with peaches from the 'sacred peach tree of wisdom.' Master Oogway finds him, and gets him talking about what's happening. Po reveals: *'I probably sucked more today than anyone in the history of Kung Fu, in the history of China, and in the history of sucking.'*

This phrase stuck with me. I have found myself using similar phrases at times. Do any of these sound familiar to you:

- *'I really don't think I was cut out for this. I am making a fool of myself.'*
- *'Why did I ever think I could do this? I don't know what I am doing.'*
- *'Did I really say that? They must think I am a complete idiot.'*
- *'If they haven't worked it out already, then they are soon going to work out that I am not up to this.'*

We are only saying to ourselves: I suck.

The impact of the I suck story

The challenge of the I suck stories is their stickiness. It's easier to put ourselves down than to build ourselves up. So, we see the movie preview train wreck and we play it on repeat. We ruminate. Over and over. We get stuck; stuck in I suck. Yuck.

Over time, what happens is that we begin to suck – for real. We get stuck in a story that becomes self-fulfilling. We repeat, rather than learn, from the experience of 'sucking.' For example, we worry that people will judge us if we speak up. So, we don't. We worry that we will look like an idiot if we ask a question. So, we don't. We worry that what we have is not perfect, and so we hold off. We hold back; we wait. And then, we fail to deliver. The I suck stories can be so sticky that we just don't know how to stand up straight again to get out of the mud.

Evidence of I suck

We tend to filter out evidence to the contrary when we are stuck. Confirmation bias then affirms what we believe. Confirmation bias is when our subconscious looks for evidence that what we believe exists. It actively filters out the stories which suggest otherwise. So, we only see the evidence that corroborates our story. Our brain doubles down and hurts us – not just with the story it plays on repeat, but in seeking out evidence to confirm our suspicions.

What this means is that we store up other stories about how we suck. We ignore the stories that would shine a light on why we may have been appointed to the role in the first place. Dragon warrior, human resources manager or general manager: whatever the role, you were appointed because someone believed in you. Perhaps not everyone, just like with Po; but, someone. The question is really whether or not you back yourself.

Does everyone get stuck?

In a word, yes. Everyone gets stuck in 'I suck' from time to time. We filter out the evidence that others can be stuck in their own stories too – their own internal narratives of 'I suck.' This is a common theme with seasoned executives and new leaders alike. We can all fall prey to the sticky I suck story.

I hear the same stories from my clients and have for some time. Clients tell me: *'I feel like I'm not up to it. I feel like everybody else knows what they're doing but I just don't know what I'm doing. I feel like I'm not cut out for this role.'* There's a kind of pain in my heart whenever I hear these stories. I know from personal experience what that feels like. And, I know how tricky it can be to get out of the story.

I told myself an I suck story long enough to have me burn-out, ultimately fail and then escape a role that I was (in hindsight) more than capable of performing – that is, of course, if I had managed to get myself unstuck. I'll tell you more about my experience later, but for now, I want to talk about the link between evidence and feedback.

Feedback: Fact or fiction?

A key theme in employee surveys over the last few years is the need for more feedback. Better feedback, feedback that helps identify areas for improvement and feedback that makes employees feel valued. In the absence of positive feedback, we fall into the trap of filling the void with our stories based in self-doubt: stories that are harmful and more often than not, unfounded. We tell ourselves the I suck story in the absence of evidence. This is dangerous territory. It's a tendency we need to understand in order to catch ourselves before feeding the I suck story and, eventually, getting stuck.

The upward trend in the need for feedback has occurred at the same time as a transition in our economy away from manufacturing. In manufacturing, a product was either successful or a fail and such feedback was easy to obtain. In the new 'knowledge economy' we all seek to improve one way or another, but it can be difficult to judge what improvement looks like or where to get helpful feedback. This transition has occurred at the same time as a transition to the use of social media. Here we can get immediate feedback by way of 'likes', shares and comments; or, we receive an absence of the same. It's all feedback.

Feedback comes in a variety of forms. Effective feedback, however, is feedback that is accurate and truly enables us to grow. It can be rare and hard to find.

The challenge is that feedback is everywhere. So, we can easily pick up the unhelpful feedback through our confirmation-bias filter. We get feedback from someone who smiles at us or someone who doesn't smile at us. We get feedback from someone who says, 'Great work', whether or not they meant it. We get feedback from the person who says, 'I don't agree with you'. (And, we can make that mean all sorts of things.) We take an email as feedback, even though it hasn't been returned. The call that hasn't been returned. The social media comment or post that isn't 'liked'.

As humans, we don't filter our feedback in an effective way. We don't test out feedback as fact or fiction. We take all feedback as if it means something about us personally – often in a negative narrative sense. By way of confirmation bias, we connect these little bits of feedback to our story, which is our I suck story.

If someone doesn't smile at us in the morning, doesn't acknowledge us, or doesn't reply to our email, then we start to play the negative narrative of thinking: 'Oh my God. They mustn't believe that I can do what I do.' Or, 'They really think that I'm failing at this job.' Or, 'They really think I am an idiot.' Whatever narrative we are telling ourselves, we use that tiny bit of 'feedback' as evidence that our I suck story is accurate.

After 40 years of research in classrooms, Professor Graham Nuthall – author of *The Hidden Lives of Learners* – identified that 80% of verbal feedback students receive is from other students. And, most of this feedback is incorrect. 'Well done.' 'I don't think that's right.' 'This is how you do it.' All of this is feedback; most of the time it's wrong.

In my experience, the same is true in the workplace. We receive so many forms of feedback, verbal and otherwise; formal and informal. Some of this is accurate, helpful and effective. The vast majority is unhelpful and sometimes harmful. This is particularly true when it confirms our biased negative narrative of I suck.

We need to learn how to filter the unhelpful feedback, seek the feedback that matters, and recognise the difference between the two. Then, our I suck stories are challenged rather than charged.

Can the I suck story lead to self-confidence?
This book is about building self-confidence, and so it might seem counter-intuitive to focus first on I suck stories. But here's the

thing: if we don't recognise what we are telling ourselves, then we are going to think that the mud in which we are stuck is real rather than imagined.

The negative narrative is just a story. For now. We risk it becoming our reality if we don't recognise the story for what it is.

The story we tell ourselves becomes the story we tell others; and, over time, it becomes the story others see. Whether we realise it or not, and whether we want them to or not, it comes out subconsciously. It comes out in how we hold ourselves. It comes out in regard to what we contribute in meetings (or don't). It comes out in what we deliver (or don't).

New leaders often focus on communication: communication with their team, with their boss, with their peers, with the wider organisation and with key external stakeholders. This is important; no question. At the same time, what is critical as a starting point is how we communicate with ourselves. If we are unclear on our internal narrative, we will struggle to communicate in a way that is clear, congruent and connected – regardless of the audience.

Start with identifying the stories that need cleaning up. It's a little like getting rid of cobwebs. Give your subconscious a spring clean to get rid of the I suck stories. They will come back, just like dust and cobwebs. But the cleaner you are when you start a new leadership role, the easier it is to identify the early signs of the story coming back. So, start with getting clear on where the I suck narrative currently exists. That is critical. If you fail to do this, you will end up communicating in a way that is inauthentic and incongruous. Overall, it projects the story you really don't want others to see.

Remember that the words you use to communicate only provide a small portion of how that communication is received. The tone you use, the body language you display, and the very nature in which you communicate tells part of the story. You may subconsciously tell a story of I suck if you are not managing your internal narrative.

Henry Ford was a founder of the Ford Motor Company, a pioneer and a futurist back in the late 1800s. He is believed to have said (or at least said something like): *'If you think you can do a thing or think you can't do a thing, you're right.'*

You can set yourself up to fail when you tell yourself the I suck story. It becomes self-fulfilling. So, step one on the path to self-confidence is identifying the I suck stories. Step two is the spring clean. Step three is replacing the story. We will cover steps two and three later in the book. For now, take some time to reflect on the stories you say about yourself. Start to uncover the I suck stories.

I used to tell myself that I sucked at running. I grew up asthmatic and was never really that athletic. I carried my Ventolin puffer wherever I went. I never trained in running. I often came close to last in school races. It just wasn't my thing; that was how I justified the I suck story.

Then, one night I was challenged by a friend to run a fun-run. It was a bet and, admittedly, I had consumed a few champagnes at the time! I agreed to something that I may never have agreed to while sober. The challenge was that if I ran a five-kilometre fun-run, then my husband, Tim, would run a half marathon – something this mutual friend of ours knew he had been wanting to do for some time. He just needed an extra nudge. So, I agreed. I trained a few times and I found it really hard. I managed to cover about three kilometres at most in my training runs. I was still very much stop and start. It's safe to say that, while I was out there 'running,' an internal story played in my mind: 'This is really not me. I suck at running.'

Then, the night before the fun-run, Tim changed the rules on me. He said that I needed to run the entire five kilometres without stopping. Otherwise, he didn't need to worry about the half-marathon. Well, suddenly the story in my mind was replaced with a 'I will show you! I know you want to do this half-marathon. So, I am going to do everything in my power to hold up my part of the bargain.'

And I did. I ran. A full five kilometres. Without stopping.

I still remember running across the finish line, nearly staggering it's safe to say, but nonetheless still running. Kirsty, our friend, was there to cheer us on throughout the race. She looked at me, saying, 'Look at you. You're a runner.' Wow. I have tears in my eyes just remembering that story.

In one moment, my narrative changed. Suddenly, I LOVED running. Ridiculous. I had missed out on 30 years of running due to thinking it was just not my thing!

Smiling in the face of I suck

When we recognise the I suck story, we have the opportunity to test it out. When I work with my coaching clients, I love seeing their light bulb moments where they realise they don't suck. They smile at the face of I suck because they realise they don't suck at all.

I suck stories tend to be such isolated, small examples of something we did wrong. Or, these stories are something that just didn't work out as we had planned it, such as a single conversation or meeting that didn't go as planned. When we nail it down from where this I suck story came, we have these moments of clarity where we say, 'Oh, that's all that is. It's just that story on repeat.'

One of my clients, a highly-capable and amazing individual, recently fell foul of an I suck story. She was coming up to a performance review and felt concerned about it, feeling as if she hadn't received very much feedback from her boss. She had inferred that, as a result, she was now heading into a poor review. In truth, she had filtered out the positive while focusing on the absence of feedback to infer a negative appraisal.

We discussed what she had delivered, the work to which she had committed and what she had achieved. On most measures, she had excelled: she had delivered what she needed to and she had a highly engaged team. She was liked and respected both internally and externally. We pulled out some examples of where she had received feedback, and the feedback was exceptional.

Her evidence of things not going well was the absence of feedback (or her perception of an absence of feedback). And, it included one conversation that had not gone well. One conversation can be all it takes to get stuck in I suck.

When we broke down that conversation, she was able to recognise that the conversation was not all bad. Her boss had acknowledged her great work at the start of the meeting. She was able to see she couldn't be sure what her boss was really thinking, and so she was also able to recognise the narrative she had chosen. She had placed this narrative over the words and actions which formed the conversation. She acknowledged that she had made the conversation mean so much more than it did. In fact, there was a double-edged challenge here for this leader, and a very common one:

- She perceived her boss as being all-knowing (the perfect leader); and
- She wanted to be perceived as all-knowing (the perfect leader) herself.

The challenge? The perfect leader does not exist. Alas, we are all human beings and not superheroes. So, she was holding a conversation with a fictional leader rather than the real leader sitting across from her.

This fictional leader is one I thought I knew well, so well in fact, that I thought she was real. Let me explain.

Feedback loops that help and hinder

After university, I worked as an employment and workplace-relations lawyer in a law firm. I loved employment law. In my eyes, employment law enabled workplace change for the better. I still feel that way. I was lucky enough to work with clients who wanted to use the law for good – not evil. Employers could see the need to do more than just comply with the law. They wanted their workplaces to be ahead of the game. I left the law firm some years later, joining the corporate world as an in-house industrial relations manager. I got a reputation for getting things done, great service delivery and for improving how teams functioned. My entry ticket was knowing the law, but the work I did was mostly about improving service delivery and how people worked together. As a consequence, I was thrown new challenges: managing other teams which included the payroll team, a customer-care team and then the human resources team.

All the transitions into other teams were bumpy and challenging, yet also fulfilling and successful. The move to human resources, however, was just plain awful.

There were three reasons for this:

1. I was painfully aware that my appointment was not unanimously supported.
2. Those that had not supported my appointment had openly judged me as ill-equipped for the role.
3. This judgement confirmed my deeply held doubts about myself. I wasn't equipped and didn't know how to handle this role; so, I was not ready for it.

What made the biggest difference to my confidence? What I told myself: the I suck story. This story filtered the feedback so effectively that I failed to act as I knew I needed to act. I couldn't do the things I knew I must. Rather, I shied away. I played small. I felt small. I didn't stand tall because I felt like I sucked.

My I suck story became self-fulfilling. My performance started to suck. I didn't have the conversations I needed to have. I didn't look after myself physically or mentally. I failed to focus on what I needed to deliver. I got stuck. Completely stuck in I suck.

Luckily for me, I have also had the opposite experience: the feeling of being supported in a role. I have had a positive narrative fed to me rather than evidence for my negative narrative.

I was a junior lawyer when I joined Mark's team, but he did not treat me as 'junior.' He had a confidence in me that far exceeded the confidence I had in myself at the time. He appreciated my professional experience, which I had down-played. Prior to that role, I had been stuck in looking for evidence that *I sucked* as a lawyer. Seriously. Suddenly, my boss was telling me I was an asset to his team. Wow. The power of Mark's support of me was enormous.

The scary thing is this: in both scenarios, my view of myself was determined by other people.

And this is the crucial thing about feedback, isn't it? If we rely on feedback, we're vulnerable to the views of others. That's fantastic if we've got someone who believes in us, but it can be disastrous if we have someone who doesn't.

So, is there an alternative?

Self-reliant feedback

Mrs. Morrison was my grade six teacher, and Mrs. Morrison was just wonderful. Without question, she was one of my favourite primary school teachers, but not because of anything that she taught me in maths or writing or any other subject. No, I remember Mrs. Morrison for what she taught me about loving myself.

Day one of grade six. Mrs. Morrison asked our entire class to put their hands up if they loved themselves. As grade six kids in the 1980s, it was not the 'done thing' to acknowledge that you 'loved yourself' publicly or privately. Oh no! So, no one put their hands up. Instead, we all sheepishly looked around, sniggered and said, 'Well, no one's going to admit it.'

Mrs. Morrison looked at us all and said, 'By the end of this year, when I ask you that question, you will all put your hands up.' We all giggled, thinking this was ridiculous. Yet, through the course of that year, she instilled in us that we must love ourselves to truly love and appreciate anybody else. Loving yourself comes first.

I wish I could remember how Mrs. Morrison taught us this lesson so well. I have this memory of it being drummed into us, but that is all. And, by the end of that year when she asked us that question, we all put our hands up – all of us with no (visible) reservation.

So, what does this have to do with feedback?

Well, if we are clear about who we are and the value we offer, then the feedback for which we look will be feedback that confirms our belief. We put confirmation bias to work *for* us, not against us. Also, we can then focus on self-feedback, by which I mean testing our achievements against our own measures. For example, living in accordance with our own values.

In his book *Power, Freedom and Grace*, meditation and alternative healing guru, Deepak Chopra, draws on the metaphor of *being in the river*. I find this concept useful when I think about self-feedback. Consider for a moment that you are floating down a river. On one bank there are people who love and appreciate you. They are chanting messages like, 'You are amazing! You can do anything!' On the other side of the river, there are people who question your competence or just don't understand you. They are chanting, just as loud, saying messages like, 'Who do you think you are? You are out of your depth.'

The challenge is to float down the middle of the river away from both banks. Chopra believes both forms of feedback take us off course. Instead, you must keep flowing in your own truth, your own strength, and your own path. Both banks are just the perception of others and ultimately unhelpful. If you get stuck on either bank, you miss the action of the river itself. Let's be clear. Both banks can be persuasive and both banks are easy to lean towards, particularly if they connect with something we believe of ourselves. However, the self-feedback that serves us is found in the flow of the river itself.

The problem is that many of us (me included) spend our time slamming into each bank without realising it. Someone praises our work and we slam with gratitude into the positive bank. Someone criticises us and we slam into the negative bank, believing the worst is true. When we slam into the bank, it can take some work to get unstuck. It turns out the river banks are just as sticky as the I suck stories. And still, they are just as unhelpful – whether it's the positive or negative bank. Both banks take away our ability to love and appreciate ourselves, and to confidently travel down the river of life.

The power of stories on our river of life

While we focus on being in the river rather than on the bank, we will still be swayed by the stories we tell ourselves. There are two key types of stories we tell ourselves.

1. There are the small (but impactful) stories, like the horror movie previews about how we failed last time or how we suck; and
2. The stories about who we are in life. This is our over-arching narrative about who we are, what we believe, and what we are capable of achieving.

The challenge in the flow of the river is to find a harmony or alignment within the stories we tell ourselves, while ensuring they are moving us forward, not backward, or sideways.

The horror movie previews (the I suck stories) will have you treading water. At best, you are stuck on the negative bank; or, at worst, spinning in a vomit-inducing whirlpool. None of this moves you forward.

To avoid getting pulled to either bank, work on identifying the stories you tell yourself and the way you communicate with yourself.

This is the start. Look at the communication you have with yourself. In the following chapters, I will look at the comparisons we make and our competency levels. But, neither of those concepts will be fully realised unless you first understand this point about how you communicate with yourself. Furthermore, it helps to understand how you, unwittingly, hold yourself back.

Our tendency to live in the past, present or future influences how we talk to ourselves. I will make this clearer throughout the book. For now, it's important to recognise that most of the horror movie previews are stuck in a past or an imaginary world – something that may have happened once. There is no guarantee it will happen again unless we really, truly take on and wholeheartedly believe in the truth of the preview as a preview, and not a *past* view.

Once we realise that our horror movie previews are a past view of our world (and often far more imaginary than we realised), we can start to work from the present moment. Then, we can start to make the future a world in which we want to live.

So what happens now?

You cannot outsource this work. This is about you. This is the work that you need to do on yourself to be the leader you want to be and the leader you are born to be. This is about being absolutely your authentic self because that is how you will connect with the people you lead. It's your authentic self that makes the difference.

Start with one step. Choose a day – today would be perfect. Through the course of the day, check in with yourself. This could be once an hour or less often; but, it must be at least six times. Ask yourself:

- What am I telling myself right now?
- Am I watching or listening to a horror movie preview of something that happened in the past that I am worried will happen again?
- Have I imagined something could go wrong?
- Is my imagination serving me or is it making me suffer?
- Is there a better story I could be telling myself right now?

At the end of that day, you'll have a list of stories that you've told yourself. Go through this list and consider how often you tell yourself these particular stories. Is there a story that is playing on repeat? Is there a story in which you are stuck? If so, that's the one with which you start. That is the story you need to replace with a story about how you can handle the present moment while moving towards a better future.

As an immediate quick fix, you could try playing the Freeze

Game as developed by Doug Lennick and Fred Kiel. These leadership gurus are authors of numerous books including *Moral Intelligence: Enhancing Business Performance and Leadership Success*. Dr. Wendy Grusin of the Australian Graduate School of Management (AGSM) at the University of NSW first introduced me to their work. The Freeze Game is one I use regularly and with great impact. It is simply a way of checking in with ourselves with a pre-formed intention. Here's an example.

I was facilitating a workshop with students of the Australian Graduate School of Management (AGSM) the first time I played the Freeze Game. Before the workshop, I told myself that in order for the students to get the most out of the workshop, I needed to be present (not thinking about something else). This meant I had to portray my authentic self, while bringing a positive energy to the room. My words for the workshop were presence, authenticity and energy. At various times during the workshop, I paused (playing the Freeze Game) and asked myself: *Am I present in this moment? Am I authentic? Am I bringing good energy?* If not, then I had an immediate opportunity to adjust.

Lennick and Kiel's work is about the idea of 'moral intelligence,' by which they mean living in a way that aligns with your values. The Freeze Game is great for this work, but it can be extended beyond values. It can be a game you play throughout the day, where you simply ask yourself the questions you think will assist you most. For example:

- Am I presenting the best version of myself right now?
- Am I treating myself the way I would treat a loved one?
- What am I telling myself right now? Is it helpful or harmful?
- What am I holding back on right now? And, what am I afraid might happen if I act?

There is power in just playing this game and adjusting your thoughts at any given moment. There is even greater power in writing down everything you discover within a journal. Journaling can help you identify patterns: stories in which you are stuck. Then, you can realign the next moment or the next day. You may realise there is a particular horror movie preview which plays out at a particular point each day, such as just before a meeting. When you see this pattern, you have the opportunity to address it. You're able to re-write the story if you like. I'll explore more about the idea of re-writing later in this book. For now, just recognise the narrative and see if you can adjust it.

What if I am really stuck in I suck?

Sometimes it's difficult to shake the I suck story. Stories are powerful and convincing. If you feel completely stuck, seek out someone you trust and start talking. Your trustworthy sounding board will test out your thinking. Show you the horror movie preview for what it is: a make-believe story about what may – or may not – have once happened. It is stuck in a loop of replay, replay, replay. To test out whether you might be stuck in I suck, consider:

- Am I engaged at work at least 80 percent of the time?
- Do I feel capable of at least 80 percent of the work I am employed to do?
- Do I have energy left at the end of most days?
- Do I feel like I am contributing value?

If you answered yes to each of these questions, then well done! If you wavered or answered a quick no, then unpack that answer. What is holding you back? What are you telling yourself? What would you prefer to be saying?

We must lead ourselves in order to lead others. We must do this work on self-communication, self-worth, and self-belief. In the same way that Mrs. Morrison taught me that in order to love others we must first love ourselves, in order to *lead* others, we must first lead ourselves. This starts with how we communicate with ourselves.

We spend so much time considering how we will communicate with others, and not nearly enough time considering how we communicate with ourselves. Both types of communication are important, but positive self-communication will wildly enhance your ability to communicate with anyone you lead.

When you realise it's just a story – a horror movie preview that's stuck on repeat – you are free to recognise what's going on in the present. Recognise what you can do right now. Act to change, improve and grow.

But what if you *really* do suck?

The reality is you do suck. We all suck at some things – at lots of things! And that's okay. What's not okay is to let that stop us from taking action that will improve our abilities and have us achieve our dreams. What's not okay is if we are communicating with ourselves in a way that has us stuck in a loop of feeling we suck. In actuality, we may not suck at all. If, after unpacking our story of 'I suck' we still feel that we suck, then chances are it's because we feel incompetent at something. Or, we are comparing ourselves with someone else. Comparison can be a killer; so, let's tackle that first and then we will move on to competency. First, though, take heart… you are not alone, and you are already on the way to improving your confidence.

Everyone is on a growth path. Everyone faces hurdles, curve balls and new challenges. Everyone gets stuck from time to time, and everyone feels ineffective. When we are not doing as well as we could, we will have a story that goes with that. You need to make sure that the story is one that supports you. Remember, perhaps you are a leader who is transitioning to a new role or managing a significant change within an organisation. Or simply that you are human. Yes, human. Give yourself licence to be human. In turn, you will give those you lead the licence to be human, and permission to valiantly fly their Freak Flag!

You are a freak, so be proud of it

I love the idea of a Freak Flag. I first came across this concept in the movie *The Family Stone*, another Christmas favourite. It's the kind of gift of a movie that just keeps on giving.

In the movie, the eldest son and golden child (Emmett Stone) brings his girlfriend, Meredith Morton, home to meet his family at Christmas. He hopes his mother will give him the family 'stone,' his grandmother's engagement ring, so that he can propose to Meredith over the Christmas break. But, Meredith is tight-lipped and awkward. She has a nervous cough and struggles to connect with any family members. That is, all except Emmett's brother Ben. Somehow, Ben can see through Meredith's veneer. He recognises that she's projecting an image of what she thinks she ought to be, rather than who she really is. Ben sees that underneath her veneer is someone worth knowing, and even someone worth loving. He challenges her to be herself by saying, 'Meredith, you have a 'Freak Flag;' you just don't fly it.'

We all have something that defines our uniqueness: our Freak Flag. Our challenge as human beings is that we try to conform and to be the norm: something we think we're meant to be. We have an innate need to belong. However, conforming or fitting in is different to belonging. Dr. Brené Brown, writer and social scientist, explains this distinction beautifully in her book, *The Gifts of Imperfection*. She writes:

"One of the biggest surprises in this research was learning that fitting in and belonging are not the same thing, and, in fact, fitting in gets in the way of belonging. Fitting in is about assessing a situation and becoming who you need to be to be accepted. Belonging, on the other hand, doesn't require us to change who we are; it requires us to be who we are."

When we try to conform or fit in, we risk silencing something essential in our nature. We're not flying our Freak Flag. And it's our Freak Flag for which, as leaders, people are looking and are yearning to see. Why? Because this makes them comfortable to express their own Freak Flag. The Freak Flag is about being our authentic selves. Saying 'I love, trust and respect myself.' This is who I am and I am proud to be me. There's the Freak. Fly it proudly.

The Freak Flag is our licence to be human and a licence to be ourselves. But of course, one of the key reasons we tell ourselves I suck stories is because we compare ourselves (negatively) to other people. So, the next chapter is all about comparison. Once we are ourselves and learn to fly our Freak Flag, the only useful comparison is with ourselves and not with others. This doesn't mean we don't aim for better, or that we don't test ourselves. Instead, it means being honest and clear about who we are and what we are trying to achieve. We focus on our human endeavours, rather than comparing ourselves to others – or worse – to a non-existent perfect leader.

FOCUSED ACTIONS

This Focused Actions section is tailored to help you build on new concepts and practices that will build your self-confidence. You will find Focused Actions at the end of every chapter.

These actions require you to put one foot in front of the other and start building self-confidence. Give them a fair go. The more effort you put into the actions, the greater understanding you will have of yourself. Go for it!

Develop the foundation of awareness

Set the timer on your phone to go off at least six times during your day. When your alarm rings, ask yourself: What am I telling myself right now? Am I watching or listening to a horror movie preview of something that happened in the past? Am I am worried it will happen again? Have I imagined something could go wrong? Is my imagination serving me or is it making me suffer? Is there a better story I could be telling myself right now?

Your I suck phrases

In Kung Fu Panda, Po Ping felt inadequate and shameful after his day of training. Po reveals, "I probably sucked more today than anyone in the history of Kung Fu, in the history of China, in the history of sucking!" What a clear I suck story!

What I suck phrases do you tell yourself? List all of them.

What's the impact?

When we retell ourselves our I suck stories, ruminating in their darkness, then the I suck story becomes super sticky. Being stuck in the story, it becomes easier to pull ourselves down than to build ourselves up. Our choices begin to reflect our I suck story. Over time, we begin to suck for real.

What is your I suck story? What impact has your I suck story had on your life? What would you like to change?

Feedback filters

Have a look at the I suck stories and phrases you have captured. What feedback, experiences or truths have you neglected to listen to because they don't fit into your I suck story? List them. List your successes, the wins, and the highlights that counter your I suck stories.

The I ROCK story journal

Concentrate each day on a particular story about how you actually *rock*, as opposed to how you suck.

Start an I ROCK story journal. Capture your proudest achievements, big and small. Capture helpful feedback you have received along the way. Capture the small wins, which day by day add up to bigger wins. Your I ROCK story journal is about building yourself up on paper. Filling the blank space with stories that will help counter the I suck stories.

2   Comparison: How to use it for good (and not evil)

THERE'S A HIDDEN TRAP on the journey towards confidence. Even leaders who have worked out how to extract themselves from the I suck story can get stuck in this trap. It's all about comparison.

This trap is about comparing ourselves to other people. As humans, we all tend to compare. We compare today's temperature with yesterday's. We compare how we feel now to how we felt five minutes ago. We compare this movie with the earlier version. We compare this apple with this orange. And, we compare ourselves to almost everyone around us. It's a human propensity. It is so much a part of how we operate that most of the time we don't realise we are doing it.

Even when we recognise we are comparison junkies, we assume we are the only ones. Even when we acknowledge that to be human is to compare, we still assume the '*super*-leaders' around us have sorted out their comparison-junkie issues.

Let me tell you that I have been working with business leaders for a long time. I have not yet met a leader who hasn't wrestled with comparison and lost the battle at least some of the time.

The comparison trap
If this mythical super-leader existed, and if they had won the war with comparison, this would have no bearing on *your* ability to

manage comparison. It's irrelevant. Thinking about what the mythical super-leader does or does not do, is or is not, is comparison. Unhelpful comparison.

When you focus on the mythical super-leader, you will fail to fly your unique Freak Flag. You risk becoming a lemming leader (one that follows all the rest), rather than the leader you were born to be.

Let me be clear: there are inspiring leaders to whom we all look up to for ideas and for guidance in difficult times. That is okay. In fact, it's a necessary part of your growth as a leader. However, you must remember the humanity and fragility of great leaders, too. Recognise their greatness without judgment about your own. That is, celebrate others while focusing on competency building of yourself (as discussed in the next chapter) and *not* comparison.

Abraham Lincoln, the 16th president of the United States, was the president who led and won the American Civil War. He is an example of an extraordinary leader, politician, orator, thinker, and statesman. In fact, he is often heralded as the best US president in its history so far. We can learn a great deal from his example. He is also a great example and reminder of human frailty. Lincoln battled with depression, lost several elections, and failed in business early in his career. All this landed him with significant debt. The path to success is, of course, often a hard one and paved with failures. The journey of leadership is no different.

Look to others for ideas, guidance, and example. Just look at the entire person, rather than the bit we see as perfection. Looking at the whole picture is a helpful way of avoiding unhelpful comparison.

You bring your personal talents and strengths to any given role. Every leader is different in what abilities they bring to their role. Nevertheless, as human beings move into leadership roles, too often we latch onto a person or prototype (or mythical super-leader). We then think, 'That's how I have to be.'

A classic example of this happens when individuals look to their predecessor for inspiration. I've been guilty of this too. When I stepped up to become a human resources director some years ago. I remember looking at my predecessor and thinking, 'Hmmm, okay; that's how I am supposed to be.' Number one mistake: it led straight to comparison. And of course, comparison of this kind often leads straight to communication like 'Urgh, I suck.' Like me, you can quickly become stuck in 'I *Really* Suck' based on unhelpful comparison.

You see, my predecessor was stunning. Impeccably dressed, incredibly well-spoken, organised, easy to chat with regularly. She was adored by her team and appeared to always deliver impressive programs regardless of what came her way. She seemed to have this superhuman ability to look composed in the face of chaos.

My internal narrative became, 'I *Really* Suck. I'm not that amazing. I'm not that beautiful. I'm not that composed. I don't know how to do what she does.' I needed to focus on my strengths, on what I *could* do and what had earned me the role. Instead, I stayed stuck in a negative comparison with someone who I was not looking at holistically.

Yes, comparison is human nature; but, most of the time it will not serve you well. More often, it will send you into a spiral of feeling like you suck. As a new or aspiring leader, look out for comparison and adjust your thinking. I will cover *how* you can do that later in this book. For now, though, it's critical to understand some of the triggers that may lead you into the comparison trap.

The highlight reel effect

Consider for a moment how you feel when you look through Instagram or Facebook. How often do you fall into the comparison trap while looking through your feed?

But to what are you comparing yourself? It's someone else's highlight reel. Little snippets of 'what it looks like to be me.' We only post the bits we want others to see. Some people have made themselves famous by posting the 'warts and all' version of themselves. But it's still a manicured picture, consistent with their personal brand. Even when their brand is 'I let it all hang out' or 'I am authentic,' it's still curated and carefully chosen before they post it.

One of my favourites is the Prime Minister of Canada, Justin Trudeau. His highlight reel can seem extraordinary. I can gush and think, 'Wow. How does he do that?' Okay, he was on a leadership high right after he was elected, and many things were working his way. But, he is human. He too has moments of self-doubt. He too has days where it all feels too hard. Any highlight reel, no matter how interesting, cannot be our litmus test for what leadership looks like. It's only the highlights.

Our posts on Facebook or Instagram present a picture of perfection, or a picture consistent with our personal brand. Even Prime Minister Trudeau, whose posts seem so very authentic, portray a certain image. We do this because we are thinking about how others will compare themselves with us when they view the posts. Leaders are no different. Yep. We are all comparison junkies, and social media plays into that all too readily. Whether we follow the superhuman leader on social media – or we see snippets of conversations, meetings, or phone calls – it's little snippets of their success only. It's a highlight reel. There's nothing wrong with this, so long as we recognise what it is and what it is not.

But if we forget the reality, the highlight reel effect can be devastating. It's what we see; and on what we focus. We forget what's missing: the lowlights!

I focused on how my predecessor dressed, how she spoke, and how composed she looked. I cringe as I write this, but since my brand is consistent and authentic leadership, I need to tell you the truth. In each area of comparison with my predecessor, I failed to look at her and simply say, 'Wow, she is amazing. Good on her.' Instead, I said, 'Urgh, I *really* suck in comparison.' Yep! That is me. The one who learnt in grade six how to love herself. I fell hard into the trap of I *really* suck. And, I couldn't get myself out of that funk for some time.

All we see and all we stay focused on is this little highlight reel of what the super-leader looks like. What they say; what they do; how they look. Snippets that hurt us rather than help us. Snippets that we use for unhelpful comparison, rather than celebration and competency building.

Remember Po from the movie I discussed in the first chapter – Kung Fu Panda? Well, there is more to the quote about 'I suck' and it helps in the context of comparison. He talks about his five companions. So, here is Po's full dialogue with the Kung Fu Master Oogway:

Po: 'I probably sucked more today than anyone in the history of Kung Fu, in the history of China, in the history of sucking.'

Oogway: 'Probably.'

Po: 'And the Five... man, you should have seen them, they totally hate me.'

Oogway: 'Totally.'

Po: 'How's Shifu ever going to turn me into the Dragon Warrior? [He lifts his belly and drops it, causing it to bounce until he stops it with his paw. He sighs.] I mean, I'm not like the Five. I've got no claws, no wings, no venom. Even Mantis has those... [imitating a mantis's front legs] ...thingies. Maybe I should just quit and go back to making noodles.'

Here's Po, the chosen one; the Dragon Warrior. But he is stuck in *unhelpful* comparison. He's stuck in thinking he is not enough. Stuck in thinking he *really* sucks. He is stuck in comparison to others' highlight reels. The Five, as they're called, have the claws or the wings or the venom. He has a very clear highlight reel for each of the Five that showcases how amazing they are. But he ignores their flaws, their internal challenges, and ignores each of their journeys to get to this point. He compares himself to the highlight reels and feels inadequate. He gets stuck in 'I *really* suck' (in comparison to those guys).

Your challenge as a leader is to avoid comparison with the highlight reels of those around you, or those you aspire to be like. Instead, you need to be very clear about who you are: the strengths you bring to your role, the challenges you must address, and what you are aiming to achieve. Not in comparison to others, but instead based on your capability, your vision, and the opportunity open to you.

Be careful not to fall into Po's 'I *really* suck' trap and 'go back to making noodles.'

You see, Po did *not* enjoy making noodles. In fact, he knew noodles was not his thing. Instead, Kung Fu was his thing. He loved Kung Fu. He just didn't believe he could become the Kung Fu master: The Dragon Warrior.

The option of going back to making noodles was not a good alternative. It was an escape route. Was that going to see him move forward or 10 paces backwards? Po felt so inadequate in *comparison* to the Five. He thought the best decision was to return to something less challenging, to hide away and do without the pressure his feelings of inadequacy caused him.

If you are in a role in which you don't want to be – or a role to which you don't feel connected – that is a different scenario. That needs a different set of questions to ask yourself while planning around what to do next. If, however, you identify with Po – you are in a role about which you are excited, and that connects with who you are at your core, then don't go back to noodle making just because someone else seems to have a superpower you don't see in yourself. Just don't do it. Instead, recognise you are caught in a comparison trap. Don't fight it. Don't get down on yourself. You are just human. For a start, simply recognise you are caught in the trap. Then, start working on a better comparison – a comparison that serves you.

Here's a fact about leadership and comparison: you will start to suck as a leader when you get stuck in an unhelpful comparison trap. I mean really. Your performance will go down. It's critical for you to recognise the I really suck story and get out of it. Getting stuck in 'I *really* suck' will make you feel small: small in stature, small in impact, and small in comparison to those on who you are focusing. When humans feel small, they tend to make those around them feel small too. The opposite of what good leadership looks like.

Here's the good news: if you understand this point about comparison, you can make a change in an instant. This instant, and many instants to come. In any moment, you can choose to move your comparison focus to a more helpful comparator – yourself.

Self-comparison: When you are enough

You live by your 'personal best' when you are a runner. That means the running performance you are trying to beat is your last best performance. As a leader, you must think the same way. Consider what your personal best is right now, and then from there you can improve your competency (as I will cover in the next chapter). The key is that the comparator is ourselves. There is no one else. We are running against ourselves and our personal best.

Any moment when you realise you are comparing yourself to another person, stop and ask yourself this:
- Is this comparison making me a better leader?
- Is this comparison relevant to how I improve my personal best?

Then ask yourself:
- Am I living the best version of myself right now?
- Am I living in a way that is congruent with my strengths, my values and what I can offer?

The impact of doing this is that you start to recognise your humanity and your journey. This, in turn, gives licence to those around you to do the same. They will focus on their personal best and aim for the best version of themselves. I call this infectious self-confidence.

Infectious self-confidence

Leaders who are stuck in an unhelpful comparison with others pretend to be superhuman. They make everyone around them feel small. But the opposite is also true. Authentic self-confidence can be infectious. As a leader, when you are clear on who you are, proud of who you are and know what you contribute, you give licence to others to contribute what they need to as well. A critical lesson for all leaders is that we cannot do everything. We are, as it turns out, not super-human. And, the sooner we recognise this, the better.

How do we 'manufacture' this self-confidence? Or how do we 'fake it until we become it' as the author of Presence and TED talker, Amy Cuddy, would say? Well, start by recognising the unhelpful role comparison plays in your view of yourself.

When you catch yourself in unhelpful comparison, you can pull yourself out of it. You can say to yourself: 'Hang on; I'm doing that thing again. I assume that superhuman beings exist, and I'm not one of them.' Or, you can stay stuck in unhelpful comparison. The choice becomes yours once the recognition kicks in.

This takes practice, but once you recognise it, it's easy to re-frame and find an alternative comparison. Here's the key: find an alternative focus. Ultimately, the best alternative comparison is to your personal best. Still, sometimes that feels too far to stretch. So, here's another option: compare yourself with leaders who openly acknowledge they are human. Learn from their example and try an approach that has worked for them.

Victoria's first female premier, Joan Kirner, had a morning routine to get her apparent steely self-confidence to kick-in. Each morning she would 'get up, stand tall, square her shoulders (padded, in those 1980s days) and say to herself: 'I *can* do it – I *will* do it.' (I read this in a book co-authored by Joan Kirner in 1999). The idea struck a chord with me at the time. It was an acknowledgment that Kirner did not have some superhuman ability to weather the storm. It took grit and determination. It took self-belief, but her self-belief needed constant nudging. Joan was human. Sometimes she needed to remind herself she was capable. She could do it and she would.

Politicians do it tough. Most people have a 'highlight reel.' Politicians more often have a reel of misfortunes (if they are lucky), or misdemeanours and maladies. Australia's first female prime minister, Julia Gillard, is another example of someone who stayed strong in the face of incredible challenge. Whether you liked or loathed Prime Minister Gillard, her resolve was impressive. She faced daily attacks on her womanhood, her marital status, her abilities, and her integrity; but, she still managed to pass a remarkable volume of legislation during her period as leader of a minority government. I remember thinking to myself: 'Wow, if Julia can still get up each day while contributing and lead the country, then I've got this. It's nothing in *comparison*. I can do this.'

Yep, there's that word again. Comparison. Back then, comparison with Gillard felt easier than self-comparison. It was a comparison like Premier Kirner's phrase, 'You've got this.'

The fact is that comparison is so ingrained in us that to try and stop it is ridiculous. Most people will advise you to 'stop comparing.' But it's human nature, so it's like trying to tell yourself to stop breathing. Sooner or later, you will take another breath. You will compare.

The key to self-confidence, then, is to find comparisons that help you, rather than hold you back. Keep comparing. Just focus on your personal best and how to beat it. Not sure if you are getting it right? Listen to what your internal stories become in response to the comparison you are making; that may be your best clue as to whether it's helpful or harmful. Does it help or not?

When you practice yoga, one of the key aspects is the way you breathe. Comparison for leaders is like breath for yogis. The way you compare (for benefit or detriment), will determine whether you build confidence (of self and those around you), or whether you bring everyone down, including yourself.

Change your relationship with comparison.

Comparison is often shunned. It has become a dirty word (hence the traditional advice of 'just *don't* do it'). However, if you embrace comparison, and recognise it is part of the human condition (a little like breathing), then you can use it to your advantage.

Make comparison good for you!

Embrace comparison. Use it to focus yourself on becoming the best version of you. The best question you can ask yourself each day is: Did I fly my Freak Flag? Because if there is one superhuman power we all have, it's our Freak Flag.

The song *Sexual Revolution* (performed best by Macy Gray on her album *The Id*) gives us a little insight into this:

Your mama told you to be discreet
And keep your freak to yourself
But your mama lied to you all this time
She knows as well as you and I
You've got to express what is taboo in you
And share your freak with the rest of us
Cause it's a beautiful thang

This is the opening song of the movie *The Sweetest Thing*, a movie about three women who are flying their Freak Flags (for the most part) and who ooze infectious self-confidence. The opening scene sees a successful interior designer, Christina Walters, dancing up and down the hilly streets of San Francisco to this song, *Sexual Revolution*, while on her way home from work. Freak Flag in all its glory.

That's what it's about. Dancing up and down the hills of San Francisco might not be your 'thang,' but it's a sign of how willing Christina Walters was to celebrate life in her way. What's your sign? How will you know if your focus is on positive self-comparison rather than negative comparison with others?

I have something in common with Christina Walters: one sign of my Freak Flag also relates to dancing. For a couple of years now,

I have been taking an adult's mixed-dance class at my daughter's dance school. I love it. Like, *really* love it. I guess there's a reason I love the scene of Christina Walters dancing up and down the streets of San Francisco. It's a little bit of me, too.

Why is my dancing of the Freak Flag variety? Well, I might love it, but I am far from the most graceful or coordinated of dancers. My challenge is to continually focus on *me* and *my* personal best, instead of others in the class. And, it *is* a challenge. When my Freak Flag is flying half-mast (and some days it is because I'm human), I struggle with this comparison challenge. But when my Freak Flag is flying high, I just dance. Because I love it. My level of competence (more on that next chapter) gives others in the class licence to freely fly their own Freak Flags too! As the well-known adage goes, the woods would be very quiet if no birds sang but the best.

When it comes to Freak Flags, comparison is about how we feel in ourselves. Do we feel free, liberated, and confident? Or, do we feel limited, little, and like we *really* suck? The latter feeling is all relational. We feel limited *in comparison* and little *in comparison*. It's as if we *really* suck compared to The Five, or our superhuman leader comparator or, sometimes, just the person next to us.

As leaders, we need to love our inner freak. Loving that freak will enable love of the freaks in others, such as those we lead. And that's when magic happens.

Elle Woods flies her Freak Flag

The two *Legally Blonde* movies are among my all-time favourites. Fashion merchandising student Elle Woods wears pink as only Elle Woods can. All shades of pink. It's her thing. Pink is her signature colour. Elle is bright, vivacious and driven. In *Legally Blonde*, Elle lands herself a spot at Harvard Law School, intent on winning back the love of her life – her boyfriend who is the governor's son, Warner Huntington III. In *Legally Blonde 2*, Elle goes to Washington to change the laws on animal testing. Both environments are completely foreign to her. She enters both Harvard and Washington in full pink. In both environments, her peers find her penchant for pink outlandish and demean her for it. Over time, Elle's pinks become muted and replaced with clothes that fit the environment. Clothes that conform. Elle's wardrobe changes from bright pinks to dark purples, greys, and blacks.

She stops flying her Freak Flag. Her mojo, the essence of Elle, falters. Elle loses her ability to shine and do what she's capable of doing. The turning point for both movies is when Elle realises she has stopped believing in herself; she has stopped *being* herself. At the end of *Legally Blonde*, when Elle presents the Valedictorian speech for her year at Harvard, she reminds everyone: 'You must always have faith in people, and most importantly, you must always have faith in yourself.' She learns along the way that her edge is her Freak Flag.

Lower your Freak Flag at your peril. Your leadership challenge is to answer this question honestly, and in the affirmative, more days than not:

Am I flying my Freak Flag?

If you find yourself struggling to answer in the affirmative, then ask yourself this question:

If I wasn't in the role in which I am now, who should be in my role?

That is almost certainly the person to who you're comparing yourself. Now consider whether this person exists. Or are you focusing purely on a highlight-reel version of this person?

Now ask yourself this:

If I was the best version of myself, what would I be capable of doing in my role? What's possible?

Conclusion

Comparison cripples our confidence when we focus on 'the other' perfect (non-existent) super-leader. Recognise that we are all imperfect humans and imperfect leaders. Recognise that comparison to others is harmful.

Stand tall, confident and proud of who you are. To do this, look within rather than outside yourself. When you catch yourself in the comparison trap, the easiest way to get out is to look within and ask yourself what you can do in the next moment to live *your* truth. Fly *your* Freak Flag.

I'm not suggesting you jump on the boardroom table and dance. Ah, no. That might be a little too much Freak Flag for everybody. Just find out what you need to do to feel true to yourself. For Elle Woods, it was wearing pink and using her unusual knowledge of hair treatments to solve the new problems she faced. For Christina Walters, it was dancing off the stress of the day with no care for who might snigger at her shimmy. For Po it was Kung Fu, not noodle making.

Ultimately, the only comparison that matters is the one against our predetermined intention: Am I the best version of myself? Do I feel free to be me?

Imagine if each morning you walked out your front door feeling like you had the power to do whatever you need to do: standing tall, shoulders back, knowing all you need to do is stay true to you.

You will find doing the work I am asking of you is freeing and fulfilling. You can move from 'not enough' to 'more than enough.'

But wait! There's one more problem that gets in the way of self-confidence. The final challenge you must face is competence and your relationship with it. You cannot have self-confidence unless you are honest with yourself about your competence. Do not run the other way in the face of your incompetence.

So, what happens if you REALLY don't have the skills (competence) required?? OMG! What then!!

Read on.

FOCUSED ACTIONS

Rethinking comparison

List five examples of how you use comparison. Now, ask yourself: Is this comparison making me a better leader? Is this comparison relevant to how I improve my personal best?

Your best you

Ask yourself: Am I living the best version of myself right now? Am I living in a way that is congruent with my strengths, my values and what I can offer?

The impact of doing this is that you start to recognise your humanity and your journey. This, in turn, gives licence to those around you to do the same. They will focus on their personal best and aim for the best version of themselves. I call this infectious self-confidence.

Remember: In any moment, you can choose to move your comparison focus to a more helpful comparator, YOURSELF. Find comparisons that assist you, rather than hold you back. Keep comparing. Just focus on your personal best and how to beat it!

Authentic you

What makes you authentically you? Include all of you: silly, funny, serious. Write it all down.

Your Freak Flag

Now ask yourself: Am I flying my Freak Flag? Do I show others my true self?

If you find yourself struggling to answer in the affirmative, try asking yourself this question: If I wasn't in the role in which I am, who should be in my role? That is almost certainly the person you're comparing yourself to. Consider whether this person exists. Or are you focusing purely on a highlight-reel version of this person?

Now try this exercise. Ask yourself: If I was the best version of myself, what would I be capable of doing in my role? What's possible?

3　Competence: How to challenge an I-will-*always*-suck story

ASSESSING YOUR SKILLS and doing something about them if they fall short – building competence in other words – is the third and final piece of the puzzle in gaining self-confidence. And it is one of the most baffling parts. Can you become self-confident when you realise that you are incompetent in some areas of leadership? All my clients worry about this one. Competence is critical. You know you must be competent.

But I have found self-confident leaders think about competence differently. They recognise that competence is not a destination; it is a journey. They do not limit themselves by thinking they will arrive at some predetermined point that is 'competence.' They know that competence is a continual evolution. They realise that honest appraisal of their competence is distinct from telling themselves I-will-always-suck stories.

Self-talk, self-action, and self-promotion

Consider what we have discovered so far about internal communication and external comparison. Now consider whether you use both internal communication and external comparison to *downplay* your competence levels.

I love the game of netball, for example. I know the rules. I can throw the ball. I can catch the ball. I can stop running, most of the time instantly, without taking the added steps that would result in the ball going to the other side. I can shoot a goal now and then. I am a competent social netballer. Is my level of competency good enough to play professional netball? Hell no! Could I play competitive local netball? Not right now; I haven't played consistently for about 15 years. Is there something I could do to improve my skill and make me more competent next Monday when I take the court? Well, I'm glad you asked, because yes, there is: I can practice my throws, my goals, and I can go for a run. I can also do some knee-strengthening exercises. All these actions are within my power. All will help my game. Not overnight, and not to the level of professional netballer, but then that was never my aim. I just want to enjoy the game and feel like I am contributing to the team.

The lessons here are clear. Learn to assess your level of competence in any skill against your need for that skill as a leader. No one can master all skills. (Even Po had to choose between Kung Fu and noodle making.) Secondly, it is in your power to improve any skill.

Self-talk

It's staggering what we can talk ourselves into, and out of, when it comes to competence. As a netballer, I could say, 'Oh dear, it's been 15 years since I have played. I had better not even try.' Or, 'I'm going to train hard for a year before I take the court. Otherwise, I might embarrass myself.' But what good would that do? I might improve my skills, but without a game to test them out, how will I know if I have developed my game? All of this is true in the leadership arena as well. You can stand back and play small. Or, you can stand up and test yourself out, learn, practice, and then try again. It starts with what you tell yourself.

Self-action

Once you change your self-talk, the challenge becomes about the action you take: self-action. The competency journey is all about the actions you take. You learn when you act. Whether it's speaking up, taking a course, running a meeting, or reading a book, self-action connects to self-talk.

If you talk yourself out of competency, then you are more likely to step back and not engage in that subject matter. And in so doing, you miss an opportunity to learn or to showcase what you *do* know. You are unable to build your competence.

Conversations about financial statements are a classic example for many leaders. It never ceases to amaze me how many leaders struggle to understand their competence with financial statements. Their self-talk is: 'It's not my thing,' 'I'm not good with numbers' or 'I've never really understood these documents.' The quicker you evaluate your level of competence across any aspects of your role, including reading financial reports, then the faster you can continue your competency journey in a way that will move you forward. Recognise the self-talk and ask yourself whether it is helping or hindering. Then, decide on your next action.

Self-promotion

The third element is what you then say about yourself aloud. This connects to your self-talk. What you say aloud matters. Either you believe what you say, and therefore communicate it congruently and with confidence; or, you doubt yourself. In this case, you communicate in a way that has others question your assertions.

As you know, I worked as an employment and workplace relations lawyer for more than a decade. I also taught employment law at a tertiary level and wrote a postgraduate course on employment law for human resources professionals. I have a Master of Laws in Employment Law, and I love the subject. I can say confidently to myself (self-talk) and aloud (self-promotion) that I have a high level of competence in employment law. I affectionately call myself an employment law nerd.

However, when it comes to self-action, I recognise there are some areas of employment and workplace relations law in which I am not an expert. For example, managing industrial action. I have had fairly limited experience of managing industrial action in my career and have not had to deal with it now for many years. I pride myself on being an advisor skilled in avoiding industrial action. So, if a client faced industrial action today, I would seek out an expert in that field to advise me and to learn from them. If I did not recognise that gap, I would fail my client. And, I would miss an opportunity to learn and grow from someone who knows this area well.

The same is true for any area of competency: communication, strategic planning, budgeting, people management, policy development, and leadership. Each of these broad areas of competency can be broken down into components on which you can act if you are honest and open in your self-evaluation.

If your self-talk acknowledges your competence journey, then you're more likely to put yourself out there and speak up in a meeting. You can express your proficiency and knowledge on a subject. You do this not in an 'I know it all' manner, but rather: 'This is what I *do* know. What I still need to understand is this…'

Hmm, sounds like a human thing to say. German-born theoretical physicist (or brain extraordinaire), Albert Einstein said, 'The more I learn, the more I realise how much I don't know.' If it is possible for Einstein to admit he didn't know everything, surely it is possible for the rest of us to acknowledge the point in our journey.

Competence as a journey, not a destination

I was so excited when I first learnt to drive. The concept that I could get in the car and drive myself somewhere was a real mark of freedom and adulthood. I looked at my older brothers and sisters who drove, and thought, 'How hard can it be?'

So, I jumped in the car and was ready to learn.

I tried lessons with Dad. I couldn't get out of Holberry Street, one street away from where we lived. In a completely flat intersection, I kept stalling. Dad was great at many things but teaching me to drive was not one of them. Neither of us could quite understand why I was stalling the car. Next, I tried lessons with my brother. This was back in the days when shops closed on Sundays. He drove me to an empty car park and I had the chance to drive around. I got past the stalling, but he discovered that I looked down every time I changed gears (yes, pre-automatic transmission days, too!). Well, that had to stop. An afternoon of him punching my upper arm every time I looked down changed that. By this time, we all realised I needed a professional. I signed up for lessons.

Lesson by lesson, I improved. Eventually, I was ready to take the test. I booked a test sandwiched between two year-12 exams. Hmm, not the best life decision. I failed. In fact, I narrowly avoided a collision the first time I took the test. The second time, I passed. I drove to a friend's house and we went for a spin. That day, I remember just avoiding another collision. Woah, I could drive enough to pass the test, but boy! I still had loads to learn.

Mum and Dad signed me up for a defensive-driving course at Calder Racecourse not long after I got my licence. That was the best learning. I got to drive fast, and in a safe environment. I could work out what the car could and could not do. Years later, I finally plucked up the courage to do hook turns (turning right from the left lane) in Melbourne's central business district.

I am far more competent driving today than I was when I got my licence. Today, I know I can drive in some situations on autopilot. The drive from home to the shops, for example. Sometimes, I need to concentrate, for example, driving in Sydney, or while driving in a part of Melbourne I don't know so well.

When it comes to self-talk about driving, I don't overthink it. I back myself. Likewise, I don't spend much time on comparison (although I do tend to give L-platers and large trucks a wide berth. That is a form of comparison that is helpful, not harmful.)

I don't pretend for a second that I have arrived at the destination of competent driving. It's still a journey. I have never driven with a trailer on the back or a caravan, but I suspect one of those challenges may be the next learning hump I take in the not-too-distant future.

This is how simple it can be and needs to be when it comes to building competence. Every day you recognise the need to learn is a day when you *do* learn. Any day you pretend you are more competent than you are is a day you are not your authentic-Freak-Flag self. And you will fail to learn.

Competence and comparison

Competency building connects closely to comparison. Remember the highlight reel? As a leader, you can fall into the comparison trap about competence and focus on the highlight reels of those around you – assuming their competence levels are beyond your reach.

I learnt a lesson on this front early in my career. As a junior lawyer, I had to attend a fortnightly meeting that we called *LA Law* (after the 1980s TV show of the same name). It was a round-table exercise. We shared what we were working on, and something we had learned during the past fortnight. I was amazed to find more senior lawyers, and often partners, still learning. As a law student, and then junior lawyer, I assumed there was a competency destination for lawyers. Once there, you had made it. Thankfully, I learned we are all on this competency journey together. Some of us may have completed more miles, but we are all still learning.

Imposter syndrome

In my 15 years of working directly with business owners and leaders and more recently in coaching executives, I have been astonished to find the majority suffer from imposter syndrome. The term 'impostor syndrome' first appeared in an article written by psychologists, Pauline R. Clance and Suzanne A. Imes. They noticed many high-achieving women doubted their intelligence and believed they were over-evaluated by others.

Most of the time, leaders hide this well (which is kind of the point, right?). They feel they are in the wrong role. They believe they are an imposter and feel as if they are just not good enough or not competent enough. At the beginning of the Netflix series, *The Good Place*, Eleanor Shellstrop wakes up to find herself in the afterlife. She is introduced by Michael to a heaven-like Utopia, The Good Place. She thinks this is a mistake (because she wasn't perfect in her life) and she should rightfully be destined for The Bad Place.

Have you ever felt like that? Ever whispered to yourself, 'What made you think you could do this?' Or, 'They think I am something I'm not. I don't know what to do next. I'm making it up as I go along!'

This is the moment when communication, comparison and competence meet for breakfast. You can either serve it to yourself cold, giving yourself a sick feeling in your stomach, day after day. Or you can serve it warm with self-encouragement, a growth mindset, and the sort of support you would offer a close friend.

Most people take a while to acknowledge they suffer from imposter syndrome. There's a theory that more women suffer from imposter syndrome than men. In my experience, women are simply more likely to acknowledge it in conversation than men. If you get the men comfortable, they too acknowledge their feeling and fear of incompetence.

The flaw with imposter syndrome is that it presupposes a destination. It presumes that there is a superhuman leader who knows what to do; they have 'arrived.' All the while, we are merely carrying our bulky luggage and working out which path to take next.

When we slip into competence comparison with others, competence becomes something like an oasis – that is, a destination that we can never actually reach. We assume it exists because it looks like someone else on the horizon has made it. The reality is that the level of competency we think we see is just a highlight reel from the journey on which a particular human is travelling. Once we arrive at the same point, there will be a new oasis on the horizon that we will try to reach.

The point is that competence is not a destination. Superman and Superwoman are made-up characters. Even as made-up characters, they have their faults. Remember, the super-leaders you think you see are human and fallible.

In chapter two, I talked about the need to use comparison for our benefit rather than to our detriment. Focus on where you are at right now. What's your current personal best and how can you beat that personal best? What's the next thing that you can do to move to the next level of competence.

Shifting to personal best

Think of an Olympic athlete. When they train for the Olympics, they and their team dissect their performance. They pull it apart and break it into pieces to see where they can change and where they can improve. What slight changes can they make that will improve their personal best, sometimes by hundredths of a second? Every little hundredth-of-a-second makes a difference in the world of sport.

Olympic athletes sometimes seem like supreme human beings. They do amazing things with their bodies. The reality is that they are human and not superhuman. Athletes recognise this and work on every aspect of their humanness to make it work for them in the arena. They focus on the next level of training to which they need to get, the next muscle on which they need to focus, and the next skill they need to practise and develop. They rely on feedback from the team around them to do this, and they rely on a deep desire to improve. All this helps them to do better than their personal best.

A Swedish psychologist, Anders Ericsson, in his book *Peak: How All of Us Can Achieve Extraordinary Things*, tells the story of America's first well-known 'genius.' He refers to inventor and writer, Benjamin Franklin, who became a skilled diplomat during the period of the American War of Independence. Among his other pursuits, Franklin was also an avid chess player. He had a passion for the game. He managed to play with the best player of his time in Europe, spending well beyond the 10,000 hours of chess assumed by many to be enough to make him a master of the game. Franklin often played from 6.00 pm through to sunrise the next day. It turns out, however, that Franklin did not improve his game all that much in his lifetime. Ericsson notes that it's not the hours in which Franklin practised, but how he used those hours. For Franklin, merely playing the game was not enough for him to become the world's best player, or indeed to even improve his game dramatically.

Ericsson also uses the analogy of a pianist playing the same songs the same way for 30 years. The songs might sound great, but we would not call them brilliant; nor would they compare with the best of their time. Playing hour upon hour is not enough. Had Franklin identified his weaknesses (for example through feedback from other players) and worked to improve these specific areas, then he might have become a world champion.

I have worked with countless leaders who have had the hours – often years – in leadership roles. Still, their standard of leadership was mediocre at best. They have been going through the motions, but they have not spent so much time on the journey of leadership competence. They've not taken the brave step to look up and out at what's next and take a step in that direction.

Ericsson proposes the concept of 'purposeful practice' as the way to improve our skills; not just any old practice, but *purposeful* practice. This forms a cycle of focused activity, feedback on progress, and trying something new – moving beyond our comfort zone. Though, this takes courage – the courage to say: 'I need to improve.' Courage to acknowledge our human fragility. Courage to say I want to be better.

It also takes a shift in mindset. Dr. Carol Dweck, in her book *Mindset: The New Psychology of Success*, highlights the extraordinary change that occurs in our learning patterns (competency building) when we approach learning with a growth mindset as opposed to a fixed mindset. What is a growth mindset? Let me paraphrase Dweck by saying that a growth mindset demands you tune into your internal communication and shift the narrative from telling yourself, 'I will always suck at this.'

The statement, 'I will always suck' is fixed. It assumes you can't move from your current skill level. No growth is possible. A growth mindset, and the internal communication that goes with it, involves a sense of curiosity about what's possible. Even if your internal communication is hesitant, it's still better than fixed. Initially, you're saying. 'I feel uneasy, or a little apprehensive about this; but, I want to be better at communicating with my team. I am going to try something new. I'm going to experiment and see how I go.' See the difference? There is no fixed destination. There is just growth. Improvement. Learning.

Competence building takes work. It takes courage and commitment. It also takes an understanding of internal communication (Chapter One) and helpful comparison (Chapter Two). Bring the three of these together, and you are well on your way to improving your self-confidence significantly. You will be leading your team better than you thought possible.

The benefits of understanding that competence is a journey, not a destination

Three benefits come from this new understanding of competence. First, you start focusing on today and on what's happening in the here and now. When you focus on what's going on today, you can acknowledge the point in your journey and find your 'growth edge.' This is a term coined by executive leadership academic and author, Dr. Morgan W McCall Jr. It means finding the next area that you can stretch yourself into to improve your approach to leading.

For example, you might have received feedback, or have become aware that you are not communicating effectively with a particular team member. Therefore, this is impacting on their delivery. Your growth edge might be to find a new way to connect with them, a new way of either listening to them, or a new way of delivering your message to them. You might experiment with a few different ways of connecting with them.

The second benefit is recognising the internal communication that might be holding you back, or has you stuck. For instance, you might focus on a team member. You recognise that you have a whole story about who they are and the state of your relationship with them. Let's call this person hypothetical Jan. Stop and reflect on whether you can improve your communication with Jan by changing the story you tell yourself about her. You might hear the voice in your head that says, 'Oh, Jan is hard work. She always wants more and only puts in the bare minimum. And, she rarely says hello in the morning. I don't think she likes me at all.'

This is just an example, but it shows that your internal narrative will either move you forward or hold you back. Consider what's behind the story, and what the story will cost you if you keep holding on to it. If your internal story about Jan (or your own example) is preventing you from moving forward in your leadership journey, then you need to leave it behind. Leave it behind in the spirit of competence building.

The last benefit of understanding competence as a journey is that you can start to make more helpful and accurate comparisons. Look at what's going on today, rather than the destination or where you think someone else might be. Competence building is all about the small actions you can take today on your leadership journey.

Let's consider Jan, our hypothetical team member, once more. Today's action might be to smile at her and say a quick hello in the morning. Tomorrow you might ask about her weekend. The next day, you may have a conversation. In fact, today's action may be even smaller. Find a replacement for your internal story about Jan. For example, shift your story from 'I don't think she likes me' to 'I need to find a way to connect with Jan better. I don't think she knows me very well; and, that could be getting in the way of effective communication.'

Remember that self-talk is just the stories we tell ourselves, as well as stories we collect along the way. Rarely, if ever, do these pass a test for veracity.

I'm incompetent

Oh, so perhaps you hoped this chapter wouldn't talk about incompetence? Well, I would love to gloss over it, just as most of us would. It's the nature of incompetence, but we need to sit with this awhile to move along our journey of competence.

As leaders, we can either focus on comparison with non-existent perfect leaders while assuming the competence shuttle bus only picked up the super-humans and left us behind. Or we can breathe, acknowledge where we are today, and take action that moves us forward. Away from incompetence and just a little more towards competence each day and each moment.

It's hard work. It's scary. You must be able to say, 'I don't have all the answers.' The best leaders say this – often – and then they craft a plan to learn more. They want to find answers to the challenges in front of them. It also needs you to honestly evaluate and make the most out of what you can do. You must recognise where you need to build competence, along with what you know you can do and where you can add value today.

Eleanor Roosevelt, the longest serving first lady of the United States and an influential international activist, was a politician and writer. She has a quote which I have held close for some time: *"You must do the thing you think you cannot do."*

You will not gain competency by standing back. You will not gain competency by being fearful and not acting. You will gain competency by taking that next step. You must do that thing that you think you cannot do. One small step in the journey of competency.

Still feeling incompetent? Well, test it out a little. The easiest way to review your competency levels (that is, where you are on your journey) is to do this little exercise.

Take out your current position description. If you don't have one, then do an internet search for one that is sufficiently close. Look at the list of key attributes or areas of accountability. Go through it carefully and write down the competencies needed to meet these. For example, your list might include financial management, staff engagement and preparation of board reports.

1.   First, tick the areas or accountabilities that make you smile: those items where you think, 'Yes, tick; I can do that. Easy.' These are your strengths. Keep using them, but don't rely on them alone; otherwise, you will miss key aspects of your role.

2.   Now, what makes you cringe? Where does your internal narrative become: 'Urgh, yes. If I work hard then I can get it done, but I don't enjoy it? I feel somewhat incompetent.' (Ooh, there's a clue). These are your growth edges. Go easy on them. Choose one or two; then, write down small acts that will shift you forward.

3.   Finally, put a red circle around the competency areas which make you want to run for cover. The run-for-cover items are those you are not ready to tackle – yet. So, make sure you have someone in your team that fills this competency gap. Work hard on that relationship because you need this person to succeed. Oh, and did I mention it's worth learning from them as you go along? These skills then become growth edges the next time you do this exercise.

Check your mindset as you do this exercise. What are you telling yourself about some competency areas? Why? Are you holding yourself back for no good reason? What's the internal communication? Is it based on verifiable fact, or is it a story such as a terrific novel that has been with you so long that you never question it? And, who are your comparators? When you say, 'I'm no good at maths,' are you comparing yourself to the maths whiz with whom you went to school or the financial reporting guru a few offices down? Comparison matters when it comes to competency building. You can too easily limit yourself if you don't stop and consider comparison when you decide your location in your journey.

Remember my driving stories earlier in this chapter? Well, it helps to think of competency building in the same way as the experience of being a driver. Even the most experienced of drivers have accidents. The same is true for any area of competency. The same is true for leaders. You can't avoid failing. You are a human being. You're fallible. We all make mistakes. Even the most extraordinary mathematicians and finance people will make mistakes with numbers sometimes. You can't expect yourself to reach perfection; it doesn't exist. Instead, focus on the action that is within your control and will move you forward.

Imagine every day is a starting point. Each day you can be intentional about your actions. Each day you choose your own adventure and learn in the process.

What's next?
You are ready to act and build your self-confidence now that you understand the role of self-talk, comparison, and competence toward building your self-confidence. In the next chapter, I am going to show you how to defy the unhelpful stories that hold you back using a powerful technique to defuse their power.

FOCUSED ACTIONS

What are your strengths?
What competencies have you learned over the years which you can readily identify? Remember the position description exercise? Highlight the areas in which you are sufficiently competent, if not highly competent already. Celebrate these strengths and make the most of them.

Find your growth edge
What's your growth edge? What's the next area in which you can stretch yourself so that you can improve your approach to leading? What are the areas in your position description that need to be tackled in order to improve your competence?

Build your team or team of advisors
What are the areas where you want to run for cover? Who is in your team that is competent in these areas? And, how strong is your relationship with them? If the gaps in your competence are also gaps in your team, then who can you find as an advisor to help fill that gap until you are ready to tackle it as an area of competence?

4　Get unstuck from the past (aka the imaginary world)

THE STRANGE THING ABOUT MEMORY, and how our memory works, is that we think it's the past. We think what we remember is what happened. We take it as fact. But, it is only our *memory* of what happened. Our mind plays tricks on us. It skews the memories. It highlights certain aspects while it misses others. Our imagination draws the picture of the past. It adds detail, creating a story around the memory for a wonderful reason: so, we can recall our memories. These stories often link to strong emotions. For example, we usually remember key childhood events like the first day of school. We recall certain aspects of that memory, but often the most vivid memory is how we *felt*.

Now, this may sound hard to accept. Most of the time, we believe our imaginary-world memories. We don't question what we saw and what we made it mean. I am not suggesting that our memories are false. However, we must unpack our memories to get unstuck from what we have made the past mean. There is what happened, and then there is the meaning we gave it and what we remember about it.

Our imagination fuses what happened with what we made it mean – this is 'what we remember about it' – our *perception*.

When we fuse what happened with what it meant, we struggle to distinguish between what is fact and what is fiction.

Consider this scenario for a moment. You are a new executive. You are sitting at the boardroom table, surrounded by your peers who have all been in their roles longer than you. You are asked a question, but you don't know the answer. You respond by saying, 'I don't know, but I will find out and come back to you.' That's it. That's what happened. But what you make of that exchange in your mind may be quite different. It might become a story of:

Phew, I handled that well. I just need to remember to come back to them with the answer promptly and have those figures ready for the next meeting.

Or, it might be a story like:

I can't believe I got asked that question. The team must think I am an idiot for not knowing the answer. I really suck.

Can you see the difference? Both meanings are possible, but they are meanings or imaginary overlays. They are the stories we tell ourselves. The first meaning is a positive overlay that reminds you to act. The second meaning sounds like the beginnings of a horror movie that is likely to keep spooking you.

If you are like me, when you watch a real horror movie, you get a bit spooked. You won't like watching them at home alone. You hear every squeak. You check the doors are locked multiple times. You jump at shadows. Our imagination lays horror movie meaning over the top of what our senses take into our mind. We hear a creak and we think someone is trying to break in, rather than thinking the house is just cooling down.

The same is true for your horror movie memories. When you don't answer the question in the boardroom on the spot, you might *feel* incompetent or that you suck (regardless of evidence to the contrary). That meaning will quickly apply to the next challenge or sensory memory you pick up in the boardroom. It is a little like the confirmation bias I spoke about earlier: you will look for more evidence that you suck and that, in turn, clouds the meaning you give to future events.

The science behind rethinking the past

Nobel Prize winner Daniel Kahneman explains in his book *Thinking Fast and Slow* the concepts of system one thinking (fast thinking) and system two thinking (slow thinking). Kahneman says that the aim of system one thinking is to 'maintain and update a model of your personal world which represents what is normal in it.' We interpret our experiences using our system one thinking, while adding to – or updating – our model.

When we become aware of system one thinking, we can shift gears into system two thinking. This is when we test out our perception and assumptions. We test out the fiction by bringing ourselves back to the present. This moment. Then, we work from here, rather than from a fictional, imaginary point in the past. Let me explain.

Remember the boardroom scene? The experience of this meeting can play on repeat in your mind. It might wake you up in the middle of the night, or it might play like a horror movie preview as you walk into your next boardroom meeting.

My personal horror movie repeat

My most horrific work-related movie still plays on my mind at times. It involved an interview in Zurich, Switzerland. Here's how it goes. A company flew me to Zurich in business class for an interview. Despite being in business class, I arrived feeling sleep deprived. I went through a torturous three-day interview process. That interview started just two hours after the plane landed. I had enough time to check-in at the hotel, change my clothes, and then catch a taxi to the meeting. The interview ended three days later when I got back on the plane to come home.

On the flight over there, I remember thinking, 'The people I am meeting don't believe I'm capable of doing this job.' My brief, received before going to this interview, was that I must get these people across the line. After all, they didn't believe that I was sufficiently competent to do the role. I had local (Australian) support, but not international.

Instead of flying there ready to present my best self, I bought into a negative internal narrative: 'They think I suck (oh, and well, I probably do suck).' Not the best way to start an interview.

Here is just a little of what happened during the three-day interview. I attended a panel interview (two hours after I arrived), followed by individual meetings with each member of the panel. I delivered a presentation with 12 hours-notice (the previous night, I was informed it had to be delivered first thing the next morning). Then, I attended a couple of dinners and other meet-and-greets with key personnel. I did not see any of Zurich the city. I saw meeting rooms and hotel rooms (where interviews were also conducted).

If I go back through the course of the three-days, I can sift through the fact and the fiction. I can recall some aspects where I performed very well. I also remember a couple of areas where I didn't perform well at all (and I have learned a lot from those aspects). What experience do I recall most vividly and easily? The horrific memories that confirmed my deeply held suspicion that I really sucked.

I got the job. This was not because my international reporting line gave me the tick of approval (he did not). But, it was because the other reporting line in Australia overrode his decision. So, in my mind, I had not convinced him that I was competent and the right person for the role. In my mind, I had convinced him that I sucked, and I had convinced myself at the same time. Not the way you want to move into a new role. At all. The fact was I didn't get the tick of approval at the global level. The fiction I overlaid that was 'I *really* suck,' and I don't really know what I am doing. Fiction became reality. I lasted a year in the role. I hated most of it because I felt like I sucked. I had lost my confidence, and the horror movie was playing on repeat of 'I really suck.' It didn't help at all.

What we tell ourselves matters. But we are often oblivious to how much of what we tell ourselves is fictional.

Is your imaginary world holding you back?

Your imaginary past, by which I mean the fiction that you are overlaying on fact, can prevent you from being the leader you are capable of being. If you fail to sort the fact from the fiction, then the fiction will win. Most people do not identify the fiction because they assume the fiction that they're overlaying is fact. They believe the past story which they're playing in their head is correct.

I had a story in my head for a long time that I was no good at maths. I had once been good at maths, but in year 11, I had a teacher who I did not understand. I felt like I was not grasping core concepts. This teacher explained everything through sailing and golf analogies, two sports in which I had no interest or knowledge. The analogies just made it harder. I remember going to him to ask for help after getting a couple of answers incorrect on a test. His response was, 'Don't worry; you'll be fine.' Now that line is a fact, or at least as close as I can recall it was a fact. But, I made that line mean something else. I made it mean that he wasn't prepared to help me. I was a lost cause because I didn't understand the core aspects. I made it mean that I had reached my maths limit. Because of this one conversation, I practically dropped out of maths. I would skip class (of course the exact opposite of what I should have done), and I told myself that maths just wasn't my thing.

Looking back on that conversation, I realise that his line could have meant something different. For example, 'I can see you understand the core components, and perhaps you just rushed the answers you got wrong. Don't worry about it. You'll be fine'.

If I asked you what you had for lunch yesterday, chances are you could tell me. You might need to think about it for a minute, but it's likely to be held in your short-term memory. If I asked you about what you had for lunch this time last month, you might have to look at your calendar and see where you were. You might remember, or you might have no idea unless you're like my husband. He has the same thing for lunch every day.

Memory can be difficult to hold onto unless we place some meaning on it. But when we place meaning on it, we suddenly overlay it with fiction.

Separating fact from fiction is a well-known challenge in the courtroom. Eye-witnesses are notoriously unreliable. Ask a few different people what happened in a particular event and each will have a distinct perspective. The sooner you ask them after the fact, the better chance you have of getting to the truth of what happened, simply by piecing together each of their stories. However, you must pull apart the fictional overlay (the story) from what happened (the fact).

I attended a Passover celebration with a few family members last year. Having been brought up Catholic, the Passover was not something I celebrated as a tradition. However, my brother introduced a Passover celebration with family and friends as a new tradition. This was the second time my brother had hosted the celebration, and I had not been there the year before. Late in the evening, my mother and two of my siblings reflected on the celebration of the previous year. They were comparing the differences and similarities. Of the three of them, they had completely different memories of what had occurred at the earlier celebration. It was impossible to draw out the *facts* about what had happened because their memories were vastly different.

Now, in this instance, working out what was fact from what was a story my family members had overlaid was of no consequence. It was just a family event, and it didn't matter that we couldn't reconcile differing memories of what occurred.

Consider, however, that this story overlay is something you do every day. System one thinking is continually improved by the stories we add to it. But, by its nature, system one thinking does not filter the story. It does not curate perfectly for preservation. It latches it on to something else we know.

The stories within system one thinking keep you safe. They're the stories that prevent you from stepping on hot coals. You have a memory of the heat and what did happen, or what others warned you could happen. You say to yourself, 'Okay, I don't want to go there because that's unsafe.'

In the corporate environment, however, the system one thinking stories can hold you back under the guise of keeping you safe. But safety is not always the best outcome. The corporate environment is based on conversations, relationships and the work we deliver instead of hot coals. There is much more nuance, and we are far more open to bias in perception or overlay of imaginary meanings.

Not stopping to smell the snails

Each Christmas, everyone on our street turns on their Christmas lights at the same time: 8.15 pm on the first of December. All our neighbours put up Christmas lights in their front yard, and the street lights up, both physically and metaphorically. As soon as the lights go on, we all catch up on the street and check out each other's creative displays. My daughter Eleanor loves this tradition and plays a keen part in designing and building our display of lights.

Last year, after turning on the lights, we headed down the street to look at the other houses. The weather had been unusually wet and hot; there were many snails on the footpath. Eleanor does not like snails, and she really dislikes accidentally stepping on snails.

She became quite panicked about stepping on a snail, given there were so many of them. So, the first time we headed down the street, she asked for my iPhone to use as a torch. She turned on the torch, using it see where the snails were so that she could avoid them. She focused on the snails and the footpath, rather than the Christmas lights. She was in a state of fear, squealing with fright at the sight of each snail. She didn't step on any, so the fear was related to anticipation of that yucky feeling you have after crunching a snail's shell.

Halfway down the street, we ran into our neighbours who had a new dog, Daisy. Eleanor asked whether she could keep walking with them and Daisy. I said, 'Of course.' She handed the iPhone over, and walked away without thinking about snails, looking up at the Christmas lights with Daisy by her side. There were no more squeals. There was no more fear. She was in the present moment, rather than the imaginary past or projected scary future.

Eleanor has a sense of what it means to step on a snail and how revolting that might be. That prevented her from enjoying the Christmas lights and enjoying the street. She was fine once distracted from this narrative. Her 'horror movie' paused, and she could move forward.

The challenge for us all is finding what story is playing in our mind. What's the story you are telling yourself that might be holding you back? What's the fact of it, what's the fiction of it, and is it serving you?

Now, not all stories are bad. The reality is some stories do serve us. Some stories protect us, and there are also some stories that build us up. It's just that when it comes to questions of confidence, most of our stories tend to be I suck stories.

How do I know if I am stuck?

There are three ways we can recognise a negative narrative in which we might be stuck. The three signs to look for are:

- Pre-procrastination (AKA avoidance). This is how we avoid the uncomfortable feeling of procrastinating. You will notice this as side-stepping a challenge. For example, you might dodge an opportunity to present because you feel that you suck at public speaking.
- Procrastination. You delay starting or completing a piece of work because you feel incompetent. You tell yourself, 'I suck, so I will just wait until I [magically] feel like I don't suck.'
- Panic. A sick feeling in your gut when you know you must deliver, but you feel that it and you totally suck.

I remember distinctly as a junior lawyer being scared of the phone. I had a heart-racing moment whenever the phone rang. I would worry about what the caller was going to ask me, and what would happen if I couldn't answer it. Unsurprisingly, I was eventually asked a question that I couldn't answer. This one conversation when I felt caught out told me that I sucked. The fact of the matter was simple: I didn't know the answer. The fiction of the matter was a story: I felt like I had failed the 'lawyer test.' I sucked because I didn't handle the call well. (I cannot recall enough detail to decide whether that is a fact or a fiction.) As a consequence, my fear of the phone ringing became more intense.

Thankfully, I felt comfortable confessing my fear to another lawyer who is still a great friend. She gave me some very sage advice. She told me that she had felt the same as a junior lawyer. She reminded me that the clients were calling the lawyer because they didn't know the answer; and, they needed our advice. Some things I would be able to answer quickly, but there were always going to be issues that needed consideration and time. That's the advice for which our clients paid. She gave me a line to use that helped me feel capable of answering the phone. The line was: 'That's an interesting question. Let me have a look at it and I'll come back to you.'

Just that one line was enough for me to focus and feel confident when I picked up the phone. I had my survival line. I had an action that I could take. It would help me feel in control of the conversation rather than stepping into a potential horror movie.

My fear of the phone had a source in the past. I had one call where I froze; didn't know the answer and felt like a fraud. I felt like I sucked. Sucked! After one call, I convinced myself that I wasn't meant to be a lawyer. Wow. The state into which we can talk ourselves! One conversation went wrong, and the story I told myself held me back from performing confidently. I held back from answering the phone. Luckily for me, I was able to find a solution from a close colleague and friend that enabled me to move forward more confidently.

My challenge for you as a leader is to consider what you are holding back from today. What are you pre-procrastinating, procrastinating, or panicking about? Then, ask yourself why. What is the story that you have tangled up in your memory of the past? What are you telling yourself that is stopping you from being all you are capable of being? Then consider who you can talk to, in order to gain a different perspective or an alternative way to manage the panic or procrastination. Asking a friend, colleague or trusted advisor often reveals that you are not alone in your fear. Others have been there before.

Start from nothing when you talk to people

I completed a personal development course in my early twenties called the Landmark Forum. It's a course that challenged me to think beyond my current paradigms, pushing me to some uncomfortable limits. One of the concepts they introduced me to is this: start from nothing. I had to approach a conversation with a blank slate about the person to whom I spoke, as if I was meeting them for the first time.

You see, when we speak to people around us – family, friends, or work colleagues – we don't talk to them as if we have never spoken to them before. We speak to them through a lens of past experiences, as well as the stories we have told ourselves about them.

When I was doing the Landmark Forum, I had a breakthrough on this point about my relationship with my big brother. There are 20 years between my brother and me. And while there are 23 years between my eldest sister and me, I have never felt as if my eldest sister treats me as anything other than her equal sibling. My eldest brother on the other hand? Well, I had a whole library worth of stories about how he treated me like his baby sister, regardless of my age.

Whenever I spoke with my brother, I felt like he looked at me as a primary school aged child: not worthy of an opinion on world matters or on anything. Consequently, I always tried hard to prove myself to him. I would walk away frustrated or offended if I felt he hadn't listened to my viewpoint. Part way through the Landmark Forum, I thought: 'Well, I guess I could try this whole start-from-nothing concept with my brother.' So, I did.

It turned out that having a conversation with someone as if you have never spoken to them is easier than trying to speak to someone with all the horror movie stories playing, during and after the conversation.

When I consciously turned off the storytelling (the internal narrative), I listened differently. I saw and heard him as if for the first time. The noise of my stories (the imaginary past) fell away. I heard more fact than fiction. I could listen to what he said, rather than putting another layer of meaning on it. This is using what Kahneman calls slow thinking or system two thinking. It needed concentration on my part, starting from a blank slate and not filtering every word which he said through my story of 'he thinks I am a little kid.'

Up to this point, I had a lifetime of stories built up about what he thought of me. Our stories tend to build up layer upon layer. A little like a Sara Lee strudel (yum). Our confirmation bias keeps piling on the layers that tell the same narrative. Eventually, we believe our stories are fact. We have the 'evidence.' The problem is that the evidence is just a bunch of stories that we have been telling ourselves for a long time.

Listening to another human being as if you have never listened to them before is a hard thing to do. It feels unnatural. As human beings, we default to fast thinking (system one). We take a short-cut and listen to what we think will happen, as well as what we think someone will say. It is a little like finishing someone's sentences in our head. We automatically do the, 'Oh, I know this person. This is how they operate, and this is what they're saying to me.' We fill in the gaps. Our brains continually do that. The way we fill in the gaps can bring us unstuck. And not in a good way. Remember my maths teacher? I filled in the gap with something that did not serve me and, on reflection, was likely to have been wrong.

The challenge is to stop and say, 'I'm going to start from nothing. I'm going to start as if I've never had a conversation with this person before, and as if I have never been in a boardroom meeting of this kind before'. With this comes much freedom. But, you also need to be brave. You must bravely step away from what you believe to be true right now: the story you are telling yourself.

Starting from nothing enables you to connect with people in a very different way. You will shift from the imagined past to this present moment.

When I came back from my torturous Zurich interview, I had a story on repeat in my mind. Whenever I spoke to the person I reported to internationally, I had a voice in my head saying, 'He thinks you are not ready for this role. You are a fraud.' That was the horror movie narrative playing in my mind. Had I recognised that at the time – and had I been able to start from nothing in my conversation with him – then my feelings may have been different.

Looking back, I suspect my internal narrative was transparent in my conversations with him. It seemed a little like I was begging for his approval: 'I can do this. Believe me. Please see that I am trying.'

When you say to someone, 'I really am confident. I really am confident,' but internally you are saying to yourself: 'I really suck. I really suck. I really suck,' most people notice the incongruence. That can end up snowballing and resulting in a real failure as it did for me in that scenario.

Why you can't just get over it

Our challenge is that we do not recognise the story. We don't question our stories of the past. We take our fiction as fact. As humans, we fall into the fast thinking (system one) trap easily and then get stuck there.

You are going to keep falling into this trap your whole life. That's right; it's part of being human. This leadership thing and this self-improvement thing is a journey. There is no nirvana. It's not like a switch flips and we go, 'Ah, I've got it. I'll be fine now.' No. You need to keep challenging yourself to start from nothing, testing your internal narratives out, and sorting fact from fiction.

Of course, you can ignore this insight. You can keep listening to your stories. Go on as before. But if you do, you miss the opportunity it provides.

I still struggle talking to my eldest brother from time to time. The library of stories I called upon for so long is packed away, but it's still there. It's not like I can do a spring clean and suddenly they are gone. These stories are sticky. So, I need to keep doing the work of testing them out and putting them aside.

The only way to get unstuck from your imaginary past is to recognise that, most of the time, this is where you are stuck. And, it's a past that is mostly fictional. If it's a fiction that is serving you, keep going with it. However, if it's a story that runs more like a horror movie, break it apart. Ask yourself from where the story comes, and what evidence you have that it is fact. Ask what you have made this story mean. Then, consider what an alternate meaning might be. More on this in chapter eight, but for now, just think what some of those horror movie narratives might be for you.

Let me return to Zurich once more. I made that experience mean so many negative things. I had a whole story about it. Not one part of that story served me. Not one part of that story told me I was competent, confident, or capable. Rather, it was all about how much I sucked.

I could have had an alternate story that served me, but I hadn't done the work to think about what an alternate story might be. I didn't know about this idea back then. Here's an alternative that has come to me since. I was flown to Zurich because my boss in Australia saw me as competent and capable. He wanted me in the role, and he was prepared to put me in business class to help ensure I arrived feeling half-alive. He briefed me honestly about the challenge I faced. He trusted me. He knew me; the people I was going to meet didn't know me. These are facts. Sure, I have overlaid some of it with interpretation and meaning, but it's an overlay that serves me rather than pulling me down.

You must see what happened and recognise what you have made it mean. You must look at what else happened, what you have missed because of your laser focus on the negative, and what story would serve you best. Your mind will make up a story whether you want it to or not, so make sure it's one you like. We can be selective about our stories if we consciously sort fact from the fiction with system two thinking. Look for the facts that have been ignored up until now.

What if the fiction turns out to be fact? What if we find we really do suck?

Even if the negative story is right, it's only a story. You may have failed. You may have looked like a fool. You may have indeed messed up. You may feel that, based on verifiable fact, you really did suck.

What do you do then? Well, you can focus on that story and have it play on repeat; or, you can keep looking for an alternate. Sometimes you must dig deeper. Someone backed you into your role. Someone believed you are capable. Someone said, 'You're competent. You can do this role.' So, look for some evidence that you are on a journey rather than that you have arrived at Destination Failure.

Of course, you can jump off if you decide this is not the right journey for you. But, more often than not, I see leaders jump off because they have bought into a negative narrative and not evidence. Leadership is hard work and it means trying new ideas. It also means working on continuous improvements. Even if you find evidence that you are not up to the job, get specific: At what exactly do you suck? What can you fix through learning? What can you fix through building the team you need?

We will cover this more in the upcoming chapters on competence. For now, remember that everyone sucks at something. You do too. But, you don't suck at everything and you don't suck by definition of being you. Get specific and then get going on your journey of learning and growth! It is better to know what you suck at than stay in the dark. Better still, stop telling yourself you are a failure when you're not!

What's next?

Once you can recognise what imaginary stories about the past are playing out in your mind, you can acknowledge them and put them aside. Deliberately. It's a little bit like when you meditate. You can see the thoughts coming up. You acknowledge the thought and then you just let it go. With your stories, thank the story for trying to help you or protect you. Then, tell it you are going to try an alternate story out for now. You can only do that when you focus on the present.

In the next chapter, I am going to help you to understand the power of the present moment. This involves working from what's happening here and now, instead of what we fear may happen or happened last time. And, it will change your confidence level. I am going to help you find comparisons that will help you keep moving forward rather than draw you back into bad habits.

FOCUSED ACTIONS

Your holding back story
What are you holding back from today? About what are you pre-procrastinating, procrastinating or panicking? Make a list.

Detangling the past
Choose one of your horror movie previews. What is the story that you have tangled up in your memory of the past which has this play on repeat? Write your story. Challenge each part of it. What is an alternate meaning you could give the memory of the past?

Try a start-with-nothing conversation
What internal narrative have you been telling yourself about someone? Can you 'start from nothing' when you speak with them next time? This practise enables you to connect with them in a very different way. You will shift from the imagined past to this present moment. This takes practice, so give it a go and see how your experience of the conversation changes as a consequence.

5   Get back to the present (aka reality)

IN THE LAST CHAPTER, I talked about how we ruminate on the past. We often get stuck in repeating horror movie stories. Let's look at what happens if you shift your attention to the present moment. This chapter is about getting clear on defining the present moment. How can you recognise it? In this chapter, I look at what it means to be in the present. How is that different to working (and living) in your imagined world of the past? In chapter eight, I show you some exciting ways to bring yourself back to the present moment.

Strengthening the spine

How straight is your spine? How tall do you stand? Your posture tells you whether you are in the present moment, or caught up in memories or ruminations. Your core muscles support your spine. When you pull your core muscles in, your spine straightens. Have you pulled your core in after reading this? We do it as soon as we register what we are doing in the present moment. When you start ruminating or playing your horror movie preview, your core slackens, and with it, the strength and posture of your spine.

I am a dance mum. My nine-year-old daughter, Eleanor, is at dancing classes way too many hours of the week. I must admit, though, that I love being a dance mum. I love watching her dance and seeing the joy that dancing brings to her life. The dance school has a policy of closed classes, so I don't get to watch often. At the end of the term, they have a viewing week where the parents can see the progress they have made through the term. The parents sit at the back on folding chairs while the students go through their warm ups and then the class. Eleanor's dance teacher often reminds the students to check their posture. Every time this happens, I find I do the same. I sometimes look around, giggling as all the parents sit a little straighter too. That little reminder to pull in our core and to check our posture has us all respond.

This seems to happen on auto pilot. But the reality is that you can only keep your core pulled in and strong when you are concentrating. The same is true for staying focused on positive self-communication and helpful comparison. When you lose concentration, your auto-pilot preview-generating imagination machine goes into overdrive. It seems to play all the scenes you may have missed. Just as your stomach can go back to saggy/sloppy without focused attention, so can your thoughts.

It's difficult to be in the imaginary past with a horror movie playing and having a strong core at the same time. You will feel your body and your confidence slump. Amazingly, however, you can improve *either* in a moment. Focus on your core and you will improve your self-talk. Focus on self-communication and bring yourself back to the present with positive thoughts. Both can strengthen the spine – physically and metaphorically.

The spine is the starting point for everything. It is that on which your skeletal system relies and from what it hangs. In the same way, your ability to stay self-confident starts with your core; that is, what is going on inside. Your skeletal system and core enables you to stand tall; your positive self-communication in the present moment enables you to stand strong and proud.

So how do you build core strength as a leader?

Find your core strength by becoming clear on who you are – and who you are not. You must be clear about your strengths and your current personal best. You must be clear on what you want to achieve, and most importantly, *why* you want to achieve it. Your core as a leader is your essence; who you are and what drives you to change.

All leadership is about change of some description.

Your challenge is to find what you want to change. Marry that with what your role needs you to change. The stronger the marriage between these two ideas, then the easier your role as a leader becomes. Ultimately, the more authentic your leadership will be. The weaker the marriage is, the harder it will be for you to find authentic self-confidence in the way you lead.

For example, perhaps your *why* is all about creating workplaces where employees are engaged and excited about their work. Yet, you work for a business where the key performance indicator (KPI) is not people related; its focus is on results for shareholders alone. Right there, it looks like a marriage on the rocks. You will find it difficult to keep your core strong in that environment. You may send a message about how employee engagement leads to shareholder returns, but the visible KPI will remain shareholder returns. Your employer cannot acknowledge the value you provide on the engagement side in the same way. Your effort will fall flat.

Everything you do becomes easier when you get clear on what you are trying to change. You must bring yourself back to the present, pull in your core, look at your *why* and decide your next steps. Compare what is happening to you right now and where you want to go. Look at how you want to be. Don't compare the present moment to an imagined horror movie and how you *think* you are supposed to behave.

When you get clear on who you are, what's critical to you, and what matters most to you, then you have something on which to build. You have the *start* of your core and you have a way of using comparison in a positive way. Once you are clear on your purpose as a leader, you can say clearly and articulately: 'This is who I am. This is for what I stand, and this is what I am determined to change.'

The spine of the leader – the clarity of their purpose. It makes or breaks a team or an organisation.

Looking within, rather than without

The spine is part of your internal structure. So too is your purpose as a leader. Like the spine, it is hidden from view. Yet, its strength is visible in the way you stand and the way you respond to your environment as a leader.

We can see someone stand tall or slouch. We notice it in ourselves and we notice it in others. The same is true when it comes to strength of purpose. It is very closely connected to self-confidence. Leaders with a keen sense of purpose will often find it easier to moderate their internal communication, gladly building their competence. Leaders who struggle with sense of purpose often have trouble with both self-communication and competence.

Compare what you are currently doing with what you set out to do. This is of critical importance to your confidence.

But what is this illusive concept of purpose? And how does it connect to positive comparison? Well, the idea of personal purpose, just like the spine, is internal to who you are. It's what drives you. It's what has meaning and significance to your life and what you value most.

What do you value most?

As a leader, you must be attuned to conflicts in values. In fact, finding values conflict is more important than finding values alignment. It gives you an opportunity for change and growth as a leader. A values conflict is when you feel like something just doesn't 'sit right' with you.

It's a little like recognising that your stomach feels a bit stodgy because you have been slouching for the last half hour rather than stretching it out. It doesn't feel right, and you know it. And so, you act. You stretch, you stand tall, you get up and walk around. If you get the same gut feeling in relation to the work you are doing as a leader, there is a chance you are facing a values conflict right there.

The action you take in response to that conflict is like getting up and walking around. You need to act to put yourself back in alignment with what matters most to you. Re-connect with your purpose instead of someone else's purpose. Your own unique purpose.

Most people are looking for answers. Many leaders look for answers from self-help books and leadership books. They look for the top three ways to be more productive, more confident, more courageous, more connected, and so forth. You may have picked up this book hoping for something similar.

This a book about self-confidence, but I'm not going to pretend that everything will change if you do three things differently. Leaders need continual renewal and growth. Your self-confidence, and your ability to stay the course, means that you behave in a way that is consistent with who you are at your core. This isn't about a quick fix. This is about life-long development and continuous improvement.

There's a lot to like about Mark Manson's book, *The Subtle Art of Not Giving a F*&k*. He reminds us not to get stuck trying to be perfect or trying to be something that we're not. I found it a great reminder for freeing us up in the present moment. At one point, he commands, in a Yodaesque voice: 'Do, or do not. There is no how.' And this is the point. Knowing what is in your core and what is most important to you is your thing – not mine or Mark Manson's.

Do-ing is inherently easier than *how-ing*. You can get stuck in the how and ruminate for too long.

When you *do*, you keep moving forward; you keep learning. You can compare your present state with your intended state. Ask yourself whether you are feeling connected to your purpose or disconnected. Furthering your work or detracting from it? Learning or lying still?

Authenticity is a hot topic these days in leadership training. Yet, training in how to be an authentic leader can sometimes sound formulaic. That is unnecessary. When you are focused on what needs to be done right now and not stuck in the past, you are your authentic self. When you are clear on who you are and feel strong about that, then you are authentic. You feel strong in your core muscles.

Some people say that our values, or what matters most to us, doesn't change much over time. This may be true for some aspects, but others change. For example, before I was a parent, I didn't value time at home in quite the same way I do now. However, I have always valued making workplaces better for human beings. That has been a core theme of my whole life. Becoming a parent didn't change that; if anything, it highlighted it even more. I want the best for my daughter's future, and so I want to see broader change to the way employers create and foster healthy workplaces for human beings.

When you discover what matters most to you, you begin to create your metaphorical spine as a leader. You create your personal litmus test of whether your purpose aligns with your actions. For example, if you find health and wellbeing is an important value, whenever you act to support your wellbeing then you will feel strong and aligned. When you act in a way that detracts from your health and wellbeing, you will have that sinking feeling; the feeling that your core muscles are slouching.

Think about each action you take as currency. You put money in the bank when you act in a consistent way with what matters most to you. You build up your reserves and your strength as a leader. Each time you act in a contrary way to what matters most to you, you take coins out of the bank. The same is true with doing plank exercises. The longer you hold a plank, and the more often you do a plank, the stronger your core muscles become. Your posture will suffer if you do not strengthen your core.

Who is in the driver's seat?

This chapter about comparison is the most powerful point in this book. When you are clear on what's happening in the present moment, and you are clear on whether it aligns to *your* purpose (rather than someone else's), you are in the driver's seat.

When you act on what is happening right now, rather than an imagined horror movie memory, you are in the seat of power. You respond to reality, rather than what you imagine is happening.

I have a saying from author and founder of Hay House, Louise Hay on the visor of my car: 'The point of power is in the present moment.'

If you are in the present moment, you are in the most powerful position to be congruent, authentic and consistent with who you are. When you are in the driver's seat, you can act straight away. You get immediate results by taking congruent action and by being your authentic yourself.

Authenticity is your 'freak flag' – an idea I talked about earlier in this book. Authenticity is who you are in all its colour and vibrancy. It's dancing like no one is watching. It's leading like you know what you are about, and what you want to achieve.

The more you catch yourself in the present moment and check on your comparison, the stronger you get moment by moment. You may need to act right now to get clear on your 'comparator,' meaning the standard you compare yourself against.

Who is your comparator?

Leaders are humans. We're all fallible. So, even as I write a book on the subject of self-confidence, I regularly fall into the very traps about which I am writing. Here comes some more brutally honest authenticity. I went to a gala ball recently for the 100-year anniversary of a firm I worked with a few years ago. I was thrilled to be there and looking forward to catching up with my old colleagues while celebrating this significant milestone for the firm. However, as I got closer to the date, I fell into some horror movie previews about walking into the room and imagining how I would feel.

In this preview, the extra weight I am conscious of carrying was the focus. We all have challenges, and without a doubt, my health and wellbeing are a lesson I keep having to learn. It's an area of my life on which I am working, but I find the hardest to keep in check. Carrying this extra weight had me feel like I was not good enough.

Coaches need coaches too. At this time, I was working with a fabulous coach, Katrina Bromell. I told Katrina about my feelings and the horror movie preview that kept rearing its ugly head. Katrina responded first with an important home truth: 'Leonie, you are so much more than how you look.'

How had I not been telling myself this all my life?!

Then Katrina and I worked through some practical actions. I could take these to rewire how I would feel as I walked into the gala ball. I chose a dress in which I felt confident. However, what made the biggest difference was reminding myself not to imagine what someone might think of my weight in the lead up. Then, as I walked into the gala ball, I focused on the present. I looked around at the old friends and colleagues that I wanted to catch up with and I enjoyed the night – the real night that I attended, rather than the one about which I imagined feeling so uncomfortable.

I changed the voice in my head from playing, 'Oh my god, how do I look and what will people think of me?' Instead, I started saying this: 'I feel so lucky to be here, and I am so looking forward to catching up with old colleagues and friends.' My comparison shifted from what I thought I should look like (or what my weight ought to be), to how I felt during the event.

Human rights activist and diplomat, Eleanor Roosevelt, said, 'No one can make you feel inferior without your consent.' Remember what is within your power. Choose your response and your comparator.

This includes a re-jig of yourself as comparator at times too! I often fall into the trap of comparing my weight to the thinnest version of myself pre-Eleanor. While this is undoubtedly a healthier comparator than a super model, it's not helpful in the moment. It often results in a focus on my post-pregnancy ever-changed belly in a negative way. So, check your comparator and check it again. Our personal best may be from fifteen years ago, but is that a motivating factor? Our personal best from yesterday may be a far healthier and positive comparator that gets us results rather than having us slump again.

Feel the fear and do it anyway

Author Susan Jeffers wrote an influential book called 'Feel the fear and do it anyway.' This has a lot of power in it, but it might mean that you do things without pausing to think them through.

It's great to jump in, to not hold back. However, you can do a quick check-in with your values first. It doesn't take long to consider whether you are about to do something congruent with what matters most to you, or whether it is out of alignment with your purpose as a leader.

Consider my gala ball example. I could have felt the fear and done it anyway. I could have walked in feeling inadequate and unprepared. But instead, I did some work on self-communication first, and that made all the difference to my experience of the night. I paused to consider the comparisons I was making and whether they helped. I realigned the unhelpful comparison to a helpful one. I remembered that I am so much more than the way I look (der). And, the evening was about re-connecting with people who I loved working with and value greatly as human beings.

This shift resulted in me feeling so much more confident in myself. So even if self-confidence alone was the comparator, my self-comparison pre- and post- this realignment of self-communication had a very positive result.

Self-comparison takes practice. Just like self-communication, self-comparison is about positive reinforcement. That means positive acknowledgment of who you are today and where you are going. Comparing yourself to others is unhelpful.

If I felt the fear and did it anyway, I still would have gone to the gala ball. I may even have had a great night. But I would not have brought the same sense of myself as I walked into that room, which meant I could connect with everyone I spoke to that night. I know I spoke with people in an authentic way. I felt like me. I connected with people with whom I had worked, and whom I hold in high regard, without thinking (or over thinking) about what I imagined they thought of me. All I cared about that night was how I felt about me. *I* felt proud of me. My self-comparison was positively geared.

So, Jeffers' wisdom – feel the fear and do it anyway – falls into the category of 'the top three things you can do.' It's a quick fix. Just jump in; it will be fine. Still, that doesn't mean it is congruent. Congruency counts from both a confidence and a leadership perspective. Before you jump in, create a pause. Pull in your core muscles. Ask yourself whether your next action is congruent with what matters most to you. Be in this moment right now.

Author Byron Katie has a concept about being present which is helpful on this point. She aptly calls it *The Work*. I will come back to *The Work* later in this book, but I raise it now because it is critical that you know it is not easy. However, it is worth it. If you want to be a self-confident leader – the kind who flies their freak flag – then you need to do the work. You must commit. Pause and act consistently.

By the way, this kind of pause is not ruminating. It's the kind of pause where you realise your core has gone slack and you pull it in. You *work* the muscles. You engage with your purpose and then act in the moment.

Finding yourself in the present
While we are on this point, let's remember to team positive self-comparison with positive self-communication. If you feel your core slacken, you have a choice. You can go into an inner-monologue such as 'Urgh, my stomach is weak. I keep forgetting to do my sit

ups. I suck.' Or, you can recognise it and cut yourself some slack. You could say 'Hmm, I need to work a bit more at this, since it doesn't feel like it's getting stronger or easier yet. What can I do differently?' See the difference? Imagine the action you take as a consequence of those two inner-monologues. Which action is likely to be more congruent with what matters most to you?

Often you must act quickly, and so you miss the opportunity to pause and be present. But try to find more ways of checking-in through the day to see whether your actions are congruent with your values.

This congruence is not about the big decisions, but about the small actions – the things you say and do each day. It can be asking yourself the following types of questions at key times during the day:

- How am I holding myself right now?
- How am I talking to myself?
- Who am I comparing myself with right now?

By asking yourself these types of questions you are creating a pause and the opportunity to re-align; essentially, you are able to pull your core muscles back in.

So, feel the fear, but pause briefly before you do it anyway. Make sure the action is the right action for you. Make sure the action is authentic you. Freak Flag you.

Now let's pause here for a moment and remember again that you are human. You are not comparing yourself to a non-existent super-leader any more. Instead you are focusing on self-comparison, and in so doing this, you need to remember your humanity. Remember your frailty (just like every other leader). Earlier in this chapter, I covered the concept of currency in the bank. You build currency by acting in a way that is congruent rather than incongruent. Remember that this metaphor assumes you will act incongruently at times. You are human, after all. It's a matter of focusing on improving your bank balance overall over time. The more action you take that is aligned with who you are as a human being and as a leader, then the more you build up your reserves; and, your confidence builds at the same time. Congruence breeds confidence. Positive self-communication plus positive self-comparison will take you a long way on the journey of self-confident leadership.

You can change anything in a moment if you are in the present and not somewhere else in your mind. In the present moment, you can regulate your self-communication. You can check what comparisons you have made and realign where needed. You can consider whether you are speaking as if to your best friend or as if to your enemy. The point of power is in the present moment. It's in the present moment that you can act in a way that propels you forward.

This point about the present moment is critical. But you need to work at it. You need to act consistently. It all comes down to how you act and how you commit to act in any given day or week. It takes practice. Mindfulness and being in this present moment takes practice. Just as holding your core strong and having good posture takes practise. You start to slouch again if you stop doing it. So, if you want to start working in a way that is congruent, self-confident, and true to who you are, then it's going to take practice. If you understand that it's going to take practice, then you understand one of the most important points of this book. There is no silver bullet. You are human, and therefore you are a continual work in progress. Your tummy muscles go slack when you don't work them. So too do your leadership muscles.

Check your spine

Technology can take away from your ability to be mindful, but it can also help if used in a smart way. One of my favourite apps is 'Mindfulness.' The free version guides you through short meditations focused on being present. You can set reminders in this app to check in with yourself, which provides an opportunity to check your self-communication and your self-comparison.

This app has a 'geographical' reminder. Let me explain. A few years ago, I had a difficult client, and each time I went to visit her office, the app would send me a reminder to pause. It would remind me to breathe and to be completely present. It helped set me with the right mindset before entering her building.

You can set it to go off at important moments during the day, or just at the end of the day. Use those reminders to ask yourself whether you have enough currency in the bank. Have you taken more action that is congruent than not?

If you are conscious of the moment, you can choose what you do next.

Being aware of the present moment enables you to pull your core muscles in, check in with congruency of your actions, and stand tall. The past and the future do not exist; all that exists is this moment. So, if that is all there is, what do you want to make of this moment?

Imagine if you could – in any given moment – stand tall, core strong, and speak your truth powerfully, respectfully, and authentically.

Once you are in the present, you can start to create a different future. And it's that future we are going to look at in the next chapter. What would you paint as a picture of your life if you knew you could make it whatever you wanted it to be?

FOCUSED ACTIONS

Present moment statements

Complete these sentences:

This is who I am...

This is what I stand for...

This is what I am determined to change, and how I will do that...

Questions that keep you present

Remember, it is about taking positive, small actions each and every day. Just for today, regularly ask yourself:

How am I holding myself right now?

How am I talking to myself?

To whom am I comparing myself right now?

Remember: Keep taking the opportunity to realign, to pull in your core muscles, and be in the present moment.

6 Get the future to work for you (aka the re-imagined world)

NOW IT'S TIME TO GET CLEAR on your destination. What does that look like for you? In the last chapter, I talked about how being in the present moment is a little bit like sitting in the driver's seat. In this chapter, I want you to think about putting the pedal to the metal and heading to a pre-determined destination. I want you to pick a worthy target. By that, I don't mean some shiny place where you've achieved everything you want to achieve. Instead, a worthy destination is more like a feeling.

Destination self-confidence

Imagine arriving at a destination where you feel the most confident you have ever felt. Now imagine feeling even more confident than that! Take a moment to picture this destination. Where are you? What are you wearing? Who can you see? What are you telling yourself? What are you thinking about? Have you been here before?

You can work on making it a reality once you can picture this destination.

If you're stuck in the past, the only thing you can imagine is more of the same: the horror movie on endless repeat. If you disentangle yourself from the horror movie in the present moment (think about pulling your core in), then you can work on being present. That is great, but it's hard work. In this chapter, I want to explore what it looks like if you imagine a better future. I want to make it easier for you to shift from horror movie to destination self-confidence.

When you are in a horror movie preview on repeat, it's hard to imagine anything other than more of the same. It's hard to believe anything beyond 'I suck'. But here's the distinction you must remember; this is all happening in your imagination. The horror movie is your imagination gone rogue. It's imagination plus. Just as a comparison is inevitable, so is imagination. So, you must make your imagination work for you and not against you.

You have to re-imagine the future and then work on getting yourself there. While stuck in a horror movie loop, your destination looks rather awful.

You must make sure you re-imagine a worthy destination; somewhere you want to be.

The challenge of the horror movie loop is that it's hard to recognise the imaginary elements of it. We too quickly believe what our imagination puts forward and we feel like a failure. It might be compelling, and convincing, but it's not fun, and it's not helpful to anyone. So, make sure you have an alternative to the horror movie. Have another narrative that you can put in place if you're feeling like that negative narrative of a horror movie is on repeat.

Breaking free of the past

Let me tell you how easy it is when writing a book about self-confidence, to dip in and out of self-confidence! I am human after all. While writing this book, I have had to work on imagining my future confidence as an author.

Sometimes it's easy to picture what confidence looks like. Sometimes you have an anchoring moment that you can use, a moment in time when you felt supremely confident and like you could take on the world. Sometimes it feels impossible to imagine.

I don't have the anchoring moment of confidence in my ability to write a book (yet). I haven't written one before. I bet even the most accomplished authors dip in and out of confidence as they write as well, even with a firm anchoring point of past success.

In writing this book, I had to imagine what my future as a successful author looks like to get the benefit of confidence at this moment. I have had to hone my skills. I needed to imagine and re-imagine the future state in which my book is complete. I needed to be clear on what that feels like. In turn, I had to answer questions about why I want this book in the market, the difference I want to make in the world, and the wisdom I want to share so that others might find it easier to get to destination self-confidence.

These questions can help you find your destination. They can help you pull your core in and get to work. We must break out of the past by recognising the present and then resetting our potential future.

And the best bit about that destination? It doesn't change because it's not a place; it's a feeling. You've probably heard the idea of building a vision of your future; perhaps it's a vision board. This advice is on the right track. If you are a vision board person, I applaud that; but, I want you to add a core component: Imagine how your destination feels.

When I imagine how it feels to have my book published – with or without looking at the picture of my book cover on a vision board – I use my imagination more powerfully. The feeling is deeper than the image. I engage my imagination in a way that enables me to override the horror movie loop.

Your feelings go to the heart of who you are and how you want to connect with the world. When you stop and think about what self-confidence feels like for you, you start to equate that future with the present moment.

As I edit this book, it is not yet out in the world. The feeling I have, however, and the focus I have on that future feeling and the confidence I feel about the content enables me to work on this book as if I am already a published author.

Author and TED Talk presenter Amy Cuddy writes about this feeling in her book *Presence*. Amy's research on the impact of 'power poses' (which are like Wonder Woman, a strong stance, hands on hips) shows the power of re-imagining our confidence levels. What Cuddy discovered is that when people practise a power pose before going into a difficult conversation or meeting, the pose 'tricks' their mind into feeling more confident.

In my experience, holding your core is a more powerful element because of the connection between core strength and the inner mental strength of purpose and focus. Also, you can use drawing in your core as a power pose during a presentation or difficult meeting. This is opposed to assuming a Wonder Woman pose in a meeting which might disconcert your colleagues. Pulling in your core muscles will immediately impact your confidence levels. It counters the horror movie. You must find different ways of countering the horror movie to re-imagine your future and to 'fake it until you become it' as Amy Cuddy proclaims.

Finding your future

Whatever you imagine becomes your future real world.

As I mentioned earlier, Mum and Dad signed me up for a defensive-driving course around Calder Racecourse not long after getting my licence. It was a great course, and I recommend it for newish drivers. It was a lot of fun; I could imagine for a moment that I was a formula one driver about to win a race. I got to speed up and stop, testing out what my car could and could not do. A few things have stayed with me from that course and saved me a few times from a nasty accident, I suspect. One of the most critical learnings drilled into me was what to do if I felt like I had lost control of my car.

Their advice? Force yourself to focus on where you want to go –

straight ahead and on the road – not where you fear to go – off the side of the road, into the ditch, and never to be seen again!

As humans, our default is, 'Oh my God; I'm going to hit that tree.' Or, 'Oh my God. I'm going to hit that car.' Or, 'Oh my God; I'm swerving off the road.' As humans, our default is to look where we don't want to go, with a sense of dread we say, 'Oh my God. This is about to happen.'

The advice of the defensive-driving guru was clear. It is critical to stay focused on where you want to go because that's where the car is more likely to veer. Your chances of getting back to your destination are significantly higher if you focus on where you want to go, instead of letting the fear take over.

That stuck with me as a life lesson and not just a driving lesson. If you focus on where you don't want to go – the horror movie fear of, 'Oh my God, this could happen,' or, 'Oh my God, this is what happened last time and so this is likely to happen again,' – then chances are you will drive straight into that horror movie future.

If the real world is whatever you create in your mind, make sure it's the future that you want. If you're going to move into a place where you are self-confident, where you feel you're the best leader, where you can be your authentic self, then you must imagine that future. Think about that in all its vibrancy and colour. If you focus on the negative loop, then that will be your default. Come up with a new default for your system that is so vibrant and so clear to you that, when you pull in your core, you move straight back to your reimagined future.

If you re-imagine and re-focus on what is possible, then your preferred destination of feeling confident is possible. You're far more likely to act in a way that will get you there. You are more likely to pull your core in and move forward, rather than backward. It's an important reminder: what you tell yourself today paves the path to your future.

You don't want to drive into a tree, so please don't focus on the tree. If you're going to arrive at destination self-confidence, you must keep your focus on the road ahead.

Now, let's be clear. You want self-confidence for a reason, right? We don't chase confidence for confidence's sake. You seek confidence, so you can lead effectively.

So, let me take you back to your freak flag. As you re-imagine your future, make sure you are faithful to your freak flag. Imagine a future that builds upon the best version of you. Do not fall into the trap of imagining someone else's future. It's your future that matters. If it does not tap into your freak flag, it isn't real.

And let's also be clear on this freak flag of leadership – you don't fly your freak flag because you want to be a freak; it's because you must be your authentic self. As a leader, you must give licence to those around you to be themselves, to speak their truth, to connect to who they are and what they're doing each day.

From panic to present moment

When you have a clear picture of your future, confident self, you can shift your mind from the imagined past into the present moment. That is not about getting trapped in an imaginary future either. The re-imagined future is our anchor for helping us to shift out of the past and into a present moment that better serves us.

For it to be this anchor, however, it needs to be compelling. It needs to be as compelling (if not more compelling) than the horror movie loop. It needs to hook us back to the present by offering an alternative vision of what life could be like with confidence.

In my experience, it's good to be as concrete and precise as possible when it comes to visualisation. You must be able to see it immediately, feel it, smell it and breathe it. You can use visualisation in many ways to hook you back to the present. For example, if you have a presentation coming up for work that worries you; where you have already noticed a preview loop of things going wrong coming up in your imagination, then, take the time to stop and reflect on how it could be different.

If you are a vision board person, then use it to your advantage. You have done some of the work already about where you are going. Now add a symbol to identify the feeling you are after – something unique to you that connects to how it will feel. If you're not a vision board person, that is fine. All you need do is ask yourself the following questions, while stopping to picture what your answers look like:

- When you feel confident, how do you hold yourself? How does your spine feel? What are your feet doing? Are you smiling? How do you feel?
- What's happening with your communication when you feel confident? What are you saying to yourself? What can you hear and see? How do you feel?
- When you feel confident, what comparisons do you make? Are you proud of your achievements? Do you acknowledge and celebrate the success of those around you? How does that feel?

Create a more expansive version of confidence. Use your senses in the present moment to imagine what your senses in the re-imagined future will pick up. You know the line about how animals can smell fear? Fear is expansive. You sweat; you go cold; you freeze. These are all elements of fear. Confidence is the opposite of fear, but confidence feels different for each of us. For me, confidence feels like I am in the moment and nowhere other than this particular moment. Nothing else matters, and it's like the world has stopped turning for a moment so that I can do my thing.

Confidence is all about building on your personal best while using comparison for good. Think about a time when you felt the most confident you have ever felt. Picture it in your mind's eye. Feel it. That is your new focus.

If you are struggling with finding such an example, work your imagination muscle a little harder. Think of anything that you do effortlessly, such as walking, or making coffee, or breathing. Remember your imagination is already at work on the horror movie. Redirect its efforts.

Your re-imagined future is not so far away. In fact, you can get there as quickly as pulling in your core. Every step you take, or muscle you use to bring that re-imagined future closer, is a step in the right direction. It's a step that strengthens your core rather than weakening your core with the horror movie spin.

Here's an example. In a couple of months' time, I will run a workshop for human resources directors who speak English as a second language, many of them have very limited English. The content will be translated as we go.

I have never done a translated program before. Some horror movie previews have already sprung up in my mind's eye. The translation doesn't work at all, and everyone sits there blankly all day. The translation doesn't work correctly and the HR directors struggle to suppress their laughter at the funny mistranslations. The translation makes everything I say seem incredibly stupid and obvious. You get the idea!

So, I must do the work on this particular scenario to help me better prepare and to help me in the moment.

- I picture myself presenting the workshop material clearly, articulately and pausing appropriately for the translation to occur. My visualisation includes what I am wearing, how I am feeling (in control, confident, calm and proud of how it is coming together), how I am holding myself (including my core). I see a room of people with who I can engage, despite the language barrier.
- I am realistic about the challenge of this environment and prepare myself well in advance; I submit the presentation and materials to be translated in advance. I consider the cultural context and difficulty that provides. I seek guidance from those who have run a similar program and test my materials out with the people who are running the day.

This visualisation is critical. It means I do what I must do now to get ready for the day, rather than get stuck in a panic about what could go wrong. It will also help me at the time. There are no guarantees that, when I am in that workshop, it will run smoothly without a horror movie preview running through my mind. In fact, there is a good chance that I will have a few panic moments along the way. So, the visualisation – the anchor that brings me back to how I intend to feel or how I expect to be – will help me shift quickly from panic to present moment.

Consider the equivalent for a marathon runner. Someone training for a marathon must consider what they will do when their brain starts to work against them during the run. Long-distance runners, just like professional athletes, know that once they have trained for the event, it becomes a mental game on the day rather than a physical one. Their body knows what to do and is trained to do it. However, if their brain starts to play a horror movie, then they can very quickly come undone. The mental training they do is to visualise the run, imagining the confidence of feeling their body move through the motions. This is the case even when it hurts, and even when they think they cannot go further. They visualise running across the finish line, spent but satisfied. This training makes all the difference on the day.

The same is true for leaders. The mental training you do about your confidence makes the difference now as you prepare, especially in the future moment when you need it most.

Of course, if you are not a marathon runner, then you might think, 'Well, that is true for them but not for me.' Hmm, okay. Let me ask you this. If you are not a runner and you needed to run a five-kilometre race, do you think that would require both physical and mental work? If you think it doesn't, that might explain why you are still sitting on the couch! If you think you can, or if you imagine you can, then you start to take the steps needed to get the job done.

I am talking about writing your own story. Writing it the way you want it to play out. Writing it in a way that starts a positive conversation within your mind and enables a useful comparison between where you are now and where you want to be.

Write a future that's possible. Acknowledge your past and thank it for the lessons you have learned from it. Then rewrite it into a positive narrative, a story about what you do differently as a result of the experience. Where you are going from here and why.

It is so important to remember to make it your version of confidence. A personalised visualisation is about the best version of yourself. For some people that means smiling more. For some (like myself) it might be smiling just a little less! For some, it will be speaking up. For others, it will be holding our tongues and listening a little more.

The action is personal. What you see and what you do, how you hold yourself and how you feel is personal.

The common link for us all is that we are present. We connect to ourselves. We speak in positive terms to ourselves and use comparison for good. We live a version of ourselves that we have consciously created, and we build our competency as a leader on this version of ourselves. We have chosen it. We are comfortable and confident in this version of ourselves that is uniquely ours. Our confident freak flag. That is the future you are re-imagining and moving towards each step of the way.

So where to now?

Building confidence starts in the present but requires us to imagine a future that is the opposite of the horror movie. It presents a future that is about strength and clear purpose. If you believe the worst, then you risk creating the worst. If you imagine feeling like your best most confident self, you will experience that feeling right now. The future is re-imagined, and you are going down a different path.

Imagine if the world were made up of confident beings. We do not bring each other down but build each other up. That's the future world of which you can be a part if you start with yourself as a leader. Are you ready to act?

In the final three chapters of this book, I will show you – step by step – how to make the future that you have imagined come true.

FOCUSED ACTIONS

Destination confidence

Imagine arriving at a destination where you feel the most confident you have ever felt. Now imagine feeling even more confident than that! Take a moment to picture this destination. Where are you? What are you wearing? Who can you see? What are you telling yourself? What are you thinking about? Have you been here before? Ask yourself all the questions you need. Fill in the detail in your mind. See everything with clarity.

Power posing

Body language affects how others see us, but it may also change how we see ourselves. Social psychologist Amy Cuddy argues that "power posing" — standing in a posture of confidence, even when we don't feel confident — can boost feelings of confidence and might have an impact on our chances for success. Test this out for yourself.

Find Amy Cuddy's TED talk online and use a power pose as a primer before your next important meeting or presentation.

7 Communication: Using your mind for good, not evil

WHEN DID YOU LAST CALL YOURSELF AN IDIOT? I must confess here and now that I still catch myself doing this. I'm not sure from where I picked it up, although I do have memories of Mum audibly calling herself an idiot, and not infrequently when I was younger. Perhaps it is a learned approach, but I am sure Mum wasn't unusual.

Now, let me ask you another question: when did you last call someone else an idiot to their face and mean it? You don't do that, right?

Do you have a double standard in what you say to yourself and what you might say to another person? I was lucky. I had a fantastic mum, and I don't once remember her calling *me* an idiot. Yet somehow, I did learn that it was okay – in fact, completely normal – to call *myself* an idiot.

The silly thing is that I tend to call myself an idiot for innocuous reasons. I bump into the corner of the table or forget to buy milk on the way home. Or, I forget to turn the oven off after pulling the dinner out. Simple little things, and I still have this reflex: 'Oh, you idiot.' I almost want to call myself an idiot again as I write this (insert eye-rolling emoji)!

So, remember we are all a work in progress. This self-name-calling thing is an example of something that I am currently working on for myself. You will have an equivalent though, so the first step in this chapter is to start thinking about how and when you communicate to yourself in an unhelpful way.

It may be name-calling. It may be thoughts such as 'I'm not good at …' or 'I am never going to be able to…' or 'I can't believe I just …'

Now, here's what's critical about this: it's all past-thinking and not present thinking. Calling myself an idiot for bumping into a table is based on something that just happened, not something that *is* happening. So, by its very nature, it is in the past. The recent *past*, yes, but in the past nonetheless.

That matters because when you communicate with yourself about what you are good at or not good at, it is always past thinking. It has nothing to do with what is possible in the present. It is invariably fanciful thinking rather than realist thinking.

I know I am not an idiot. I am, however, human and I forget things from time to time. I knock into things when I am rushing or not thinking about where I am going. If I must name it, I am a human and not an idiot.

Remember my maths story, stemming from the maths teacher that used sailing and golf analogies which were difficult for me to translate? I used to say I was no good at maths, which is a widespread phenomenon among students and adults alike. This is past, imaginary thinking. I based it on some experiences that had made me feel like I didn't know what I was doing when it came to crunching numbers. Some events in Year 11 made me think I was not 'getting it' quickly enough. I turned those events into a story that maths just wasn't my thing.

And yet, it turns out I am quite good with numbers. I quite like using them to solve problems. It took changing the way I communicated with myself about maths to realise this and to shift to the present reality – the way I approach numbers now.

So, what are you telling yourself right now that is unhelpful?

Would you tell your best friend: 'You are no good at maths; it's not your thing.' Would you tell your best friend: 'It's not worth trying to understand it; you are never going to get it.' Would you tell your best friend: 'Don't speak up; you will expose yourself as the idiot you are.'

I hope not.

So, what makes it okay for you to talk to yourself in this way?

If you are going to shift this thinking and communicate with yourself differently, you must understand what it means to move from the past to the present.

The German-born theoretical physicist, Albert Einstein (yep, him again), said, 'People like us who believe in physics know that the distinction between past, present, and future is only a stubbornly persistent illusion.'

I'm with Einstein on this, and I am painfully aware of how persistent the illusion can be. Right now, I am writing this sentence. As soon as I enter a full stop, the moment has passed. That sentence was written in the past instead of in this present moment. By the time you read this sentence, you are reading a sentence I wrote some time ago. And while you read it, you are in that moment. But that moment quickly becomes the past and the moment is forever gone.

Or is it?

As I write this, I might ruminate on a story from my past that relates to this material, and that experience of contemplating can feel as real as if it just happened. Or, it's happening right now. I might also daydream about what it means to publish this book and to get it out in print. That can create a similar palpable feeling that is connected to right now. It's all about the future.

The best self-talk is neither positive nor negative; it is accurate and fair

Albert Einstein reminds us that the whole notion of past, present, future is an illusion. If that is the case, then you have the opportunity to make the illusion work for you, rather than against you. It's the chance to ruminate on stuff that moves you forward, rather than backward. It's the chance to imagine what's possible, rather than painfully believe what's not.

All good, you say. But how? You can start by being clear about what you tell yourself. Test out if what you think is fact or imagination.

Renowned author and speaker, Byron Katie, has an excellent process for doing this work, which is called simply 'The Work.' By its name, it should be clear that her process needs action by us, rather than inaction. Action enables us to almost immediately get clear on what is fact and what is fiction. It's not *hard* work.

The Work, in its purest form, is just four questions:

1. Is it true?
2. Can you know that it's true?
3. How do you react? What happens when you believe that thought?
4. Who would you be without the thought?

I also love the saying from Byron Katie: 'You either believe your stressful thoughts or you question them – there's no other choice.' You can stick with your past, imaginary horror movie previews; or, you can question them.

How do you know when to ask yourself these questions?

When you find yourself ruminating on a past story, ask yourself whether it is helping you move in the direction of confidence and self-leadership, or whether the story is eating away at your spirit. If the answer is the latter, then do the work. Go through the questions and start to get to the bottom of what is real, along with what is imaginary.

Byron Katie co-authored a children's book with Hans Wilhelm called *The Four Questions: For Henny Penny* and *Anybody with Stressful Thoughts*. Remember Henny Penny from your childhood? I do, though I wish I had read Byron Katie's version! Henny Penny was a chicken who believed that the sky was falling and alerted all and sundry to this 'fact.' It turned out that it was merely an acorn that had fallen off a tree and hit Henny Penny on the head. Henny Penny had not seen the acorn; she had inferred (imagined) that the sky was falling because something had hit her on the head.

The simplicity of this story was lost on me growing up, unfortunately. I always thought Henny Penny was a little like the *Boy Who Cried Wolf* – a mischievous chicken that was playing tricks rather than a deluded, anxious chicken stressed out of its tiny mind. Perhaps that was because I hadn't done The Work. I was with Henny Penny, believing it was possible that the sky really might fall one day. Oh, the power and intoxication of imaginary stressful thoughts.

As leaders – particularly leaders who believe we are meant to be the perfect prototype leader – it is easy to get alarmed by what we tell ourselves and accept it to be fact.

Why must you understand this?

What you say to yourself matters so much. You need to work from fact rather than fiction. You otherwise risk blowing yourself up like a balloon or breaking yourself down. You want to avoid both of these extremes. Positive self-talk can cause problems if it is inaccurate.

I was struck by a stark (and worrying) example of this recently. Presidential candidate and former First Lady and senator, Hillary Clinton, wrote in her book *What Happened* about a comedy skit starring her and the current US President, Donald Trump from 2006 (yes, a decade before the presidential race).

In the skit, Hillary's wax statue at Madame Tussauds had been stolen. The real Hillary is standing in for the stolen wax statue. Donald is standing nearby. He looks at the 'statue' of Hillary and says 'You look really great. Unbelievable. I've never seen anything like it. The hair is magnificent. The face is beautiful. You know, I really think you'd make a great president. Nobody could come close.' The camera then pans out and reveals that Donald is talking to his reflection and not to Hillary at all.

In this era of untruths and fake news, one thing appears to be true: Donald is a master of self-talk and continues to talk himself up – not down. At every opportunity. He is perhaps the most potent example of what self-talk can do.

Which sounds like an argument against self-talk, doesn't it? We don't all want to be "tremendous" in a way that sounds fake and inauthentic.

But no. I am not for a moment suggesting that you use self-talk to blow yourself up like a big (orange) balloon. I do not want you to alter the truth. Far from it. Byron Katie's work is all about getting to the reality, instead of changing it or falsifying it. True leadership is not about telling yourself you are something you are not. It's about acknowledging where you really are from a place of strength.

I'm going to say that again. Do not tell yourself you are something you are not. If you do, you might follow Donald down a slippery slope of self-delusion. Positive self-talk means talking to yourself in an accurate and fair way.

If I call myself an idiot, it is neither accurate nor fair and is definitely not true. If I call myself an unparalleled genius who never makes a mistake, this is neither accurate nor fair and certainly not true. If I call myself lovable and a life-long learner, I know this is accurate. This is fair, and this is true.

One is helpful. The first two are very unhelpful. It's your choice. You can believe the stressful thought of 'I can't ...' or 'I am ...' or 'I am not ...' or, you can question the thought and pull it apart.

In chapter one, I talked about the communication that we have with ourselves. We spend all this time thinking about how we communicate with others as leaders. However, we don't spend enough time thinking about how we communicate with ourselves.

This work is about what you tell yourself. Is it serving you or is it just putting you down and not helping you shift into that confident-leader mode?

If you catch yourself in a story that's not serving you, you have a choice. You have the opportunity to change the story.

The story you tell yourself

There is no perfect leader. No leader has it all or can tick every box from a competency perspective on leadership. If you tell yourself a story about a destination where you have it all, then you set yourself up for life-long disappointment.

Leadership is a continual journey. When you feel you have mastered a particular skill or competency, or when you feel you have changed your communication with yourself, you are likely to be tested again and must learn the next level. You could re-learn what you thought you had mastered.

The Work is about sustainable self-confidence in the face of the challenges of being a leader. You do this by using the four questions to give yourself accurate feedback and self-talk.

The way you communicate with yourself must be founded on a licence to continually improve and to support yourself in the journey of self-improvement. We are fallible. Our self-confidence or self-belief comes from recognising that we are human, just like the person next to us. You must recognise and celebrate your strengths and your challenges, as well as the strengths and challenges of those around you.

If you can value it in yourself, you can appreciate it in others. Remember Mrs. Morrison, my grade six teacher, who told us we must be able to love ourselves before we can love someone else? You must be able to believe in yourself and back yourself in order to be able to back somebody else as well.

The three Rs we all should learn in school

I have developed a useful three-step process that works alongside Byron Katie's work. My process helps shift your self-communication, so you can change your habits in the long term. These are the three Rs we should all learn at school!

Reflect on the narrative you are telling yourself. For example, I suck at this.

Recognise the narrative when it happens. Say: 'Hello! Here you go again. You are persistent, aren't you?'

Re-write the narrative. For example, 'I am learning a new skill and that takes time.' Draw on this re-written narrative when you catch yourself in the negative story.

That takes work and practice, but you will start to see results from the first moment you recognise the narrative you are telling yourself.

Reflect on a regular basis

If the moment of power is in the present moment, then you must be able to talk yourself back to the present moment. Say to your imagination – hang on; you are playing the wrong movie preview.

So, you engage your core. You pull it in. But your core slackens again before you know it. We are transported into that imaginary past or horror future again. That is unless you have been doing strength work on your core.

Doing work that strengthens your core means that your posture improves over time. You build muscle memory. Your spine straightens. The same happens if you work on communicating with yourself. You might read this book and think, 'Oh, I already do that.' At that moment, you smile at yourself and say something positive. However, if you don't practice your self-communication, then you won't get much in return. You might get little reminders now and then when your self-talk is stark and horrid.

Shawn Achor, the author of *The Happiness Advantage*, writes about the 'Tetris effect', which is where you prime yourself for a positive outcome or positive thinking. One of the ways he suggests is gratitude journaling; writing three things down once a day for which you are grateful. The research he draws on indicates that the more you focus on the positive, the more you see the positive.

The same is true for communication with yourself. The more you do the reflection work, recognise the story and re-write the narrative, then the faster you recognise when you fall out of that narrative and back into a loop.

Recognise when you are metaphorically reading a book

I love reading. I would read all day – every day if I could. My bliss is a Sunday afternoon with a cup of tea, a book and a quiet space on my own with no interruptions. I read for work, I read for growth, and I read for pleasure. I am a big Harry Potter fan, and I still reach out for one of that series when I want to escape the world for a little while and not think too hard.

When I sit and read a novel, I get so absorbed that the world around me disappears for a while. It's the best feeling. I can be at Hogwarts with Harry within the blink of an eye. As I read the first few lines of a chapter, I am there. And yet, I am not there. I am still sitting on my couch at home reading my book. In my imagination, plates of food keep magically re-filling and stars light the sky. In the real world, I have eaten my biscuit, my tea is cold, and the rain dribbles down the window pane.

Although reading transports me, I never question which reality I am in. I know that I am being distracted from reality. My imagination is let loose and creates the pictures based on the words I read.

It's not so easy to recognise when you get stuck in an 'I suck' story. You get stuck in re-playing past fears or worries – horror movie. And yet, it's the same process. You are not in the real world; you are in an imagined past. You might look like you're in the present moment, chatting with someone. But another thought distracts you.

We all fall into this trap too easily. It can be intoxicating; it happens as if by magic. It's hard to know it's coming. But easier to recognise once you are there. You can relive the past and believe that imaginary world is true, but you are limiting your ability to be the leader you were born to be.

If you **reflect**, **recognise** and **rewrite** often, then you get better at it. You build a better 'muscle memory' for it. Then you will do it more naturally and more often.

Rewrite the negative loop

Have you ever been afraid of sending an email? You know, you have drafted it, re-drafted it and saved it. Deleted it and started again.

I have done this on several occasions. I still do from time to time. I have an email that's sitting in my drafts right now that I have put off sending. Sometimes, I have a good reason. I might be working through the best way to approach the email communication or I am waiting on further information to complete it. But sometimes it's because I am caught in a negative-story loop.

To get out of the loop, I reflect on what's stopping me. Of what am I afraid? What's the story that I'm telling myself that's preventing me from pressing send? Sometimes the story comes to me quickly. Sometimes it takes a little longer. Usually, the movie in my mind looks like this: the person receives the email and reacts negatively. They don't like my work. They feel my work is not up to scratch.

If I recognise that story, only then can I re-write it. Byron Katie's questions can assist here too. I ask myself, 'What evidence do I have that the work is not up to scratch?' 'What evidence do I have that the receiver of the email might not like it?' I can ask myself, 'What's the worst that could happen? And, if that happened, what would I do?'

Re-writing the story involves peeling back the layers. Once you peel back sufficient layers, you recognise the story for what it is: a story that is not serving you. The story might be a distant memory; it has little if any relevance to today's email.

Turn the self-talk that harms you into a new story. Imagine the person receives your email and thinks, 'Wow, that is helpful.' Or, 'Wow, that is helpful. All I need is to ask a question about the last paragraph.' Or, 'Wow, Leonie is so quick. I have a few questions, but I'm delighted she got back to me in a flash.'

What's the worst that can happen?

When it's time to go for a run, have you noticed the hardest part is getting off the couch, putting your runners on and walking out the door? The same is true for three R's work. We don't like it. We don't want to delve into what's holding us back because we might not like what we find. Are you scared that the loop might be real?

If you find that the loop has some evidence to it, that's okay. It's time to act. For example, I don't know how to run a workshop for human resource directors whose English is limited and who will be relying on a translator. I have never done that before. Do I want that to stop me from doing the work to get it done and be proud of my work though? Hell no.

Once you sit down and reflect, you shift the narrative from a horror story into a realistic story. You see what else is possible. You get to create and re-write the narrative. You start to treat yourself like you would your best friend. You speak to yourself like you are your best supporter.

I am Leonie Green; I am Leonie; I am

I dabble in meditation. There's some honesty right there. I'm no expert. It doesn't come naturally to me. Although I acknowledge its benefit, I find it challenging to prioritise it in my day. About 12 months ago, I came across a three-minute meditation by author and teacher Deepak Chopra that fits into my day. It helps me shift from the past to the present moment. You can find the meditation on YouTube by searching for "Deepak Chopra Three Minute Meditation."

Chopra's three-minute meditation moves you through three stages: from saying your full name: 'I am Leonie Green;' to saying just your first name: 'I am Leonie;' and then to simply: 'I am.' When you say your full name, you think of all that you are distracted or stressed about right now, but as you shift, you get back to the present moment. It is one of the most accessible meditations I have come across.

It helps me remove the baggage of the immediate past and the more distant past. It shifts me back to the present moment. Once I am in the present and aware of its possibility, I start to do the reflection work in a more open, present and kind state. You can also use this meditation throughout your working day. It's only three minutes.

If you have a day that feels stuck in 'I suck,' then this is the time to use it. It can help shift your thinking back into a positive frame. Draw on this meditation when you feel yourself ruminating or getting anxious about a piece of work, or the length of your to-do list. Re-centre yourself in the now and then re-focus on a decisive action (rather than a negative loop).

Meditation is not for everyone. However, the best mindfulness meditations get us back into affirmative action. Mindfulness is not about checking out from the world. Instead, it's about re-wiring yourself to recognise the present moment.

Wake up from your nightmare

Your past will keep holding you back if you let it. Remember, the difference between the past, present, and future is all an illusion. It's a convincing illusion and one that you must recognise for what it is. Do the work to make sure that the communication that you have with yourself is communication that serves you, rather than takes away from what you could be. Return to be in the present moment if you want to make a difference in the here and now. Get out of the past to make the most of the present and the future.

Imagine if your worst nightmare is, in fact, a figment of your imagination. You wake up and realise you've just been dreaming. When you wake up from a dream, you often have a moment of relief where you think 'phew, I'm back in reality.' That's what this practice is like. You can wake up and realise that you are enough. Anything is possible. What a relief! Shift from the horror movie preview loop to a present moment where anything is possible.

When you recognise that you've just been playing a loop that's not serving you, you can 'wake up' and work from the real present moment.

Once you get unstuck from the past, you are back in the driver's seat of the present. That's where the fun starts. So, what's possible for you right now? What do you want to do at this very moment, and what would you do if you knew you weren't holding yourself back?

FOCUSED ACTIONS

Fair and accurate

The best self-talk is neither positive nor negative; it is accurate and fair. List five positive self-talk lines, and five negative self-talk lines. Now, rewrite the negative ones using accurate and fair language. See if you can enhance the positive list again using better language.

Past stories

What past story have you been ruminating on lately? What imaginary horror movie preview have you been watching and feeling? Chances are it has been eating away at your spirit. Write it down; then, go through the questions below to start to get to the bottom of what is real and what is imaginary.

Is it true?

Can you be sure that it is true? How do you react to the stories? What do you feel when you believe that thought? Who would you be without that thought?

Challenge the narrative, build the muscle memory

Consider an example of repeated, negative self-talk about an experience you've had. Use the three R's below to challenge the narrative.

Reflect on a narrative you are telling yourself. For example, I suck at …

Recognise the narrative when it happens. Say: 'Hello! Here you go again. You are persistent, aren't you?'

Re-write the narrative. For example, 'I am learning a new skill and that takes time.' Draw on this re-written narrative when you catch yourself in the negative story. Use this tool often.

If you reflect, recognise and rewrite often, then you get better at it. You build a better muscle memory for it. Then you will have created a new habit that serves you well.

Deepak Chopra's three-minute meditation

Meditation assists us to be in the present moment. Deepak Chopra's three-minute meditation moves you through three stages: from saying your full name: 'I am Leonie Green;' to saying just your first name: 'I am Leonie;' to then simply: 'I am.' When you say your full name, you think of all that you are distracted or stressed about right now, but as you shift, you get back to the present moment. It is one of the most accessible meditations I have come across.

Thank you very much for flying your freak flag

Shawn Achor's gratitude journal is a great suggestion. Here's a not so subtle twist. It's a "thank you very much for flying your freak flag" journal. I can't say *thank you very much* without hearing the 1980s jingle for Roses chocolates. For those of you who know it, you will see how the words fit the tune... thank you very much for flying your freak flag, thank you very much. Thank you very, very, very much! And my apologies in advance when this gets stuck in your head. There are worse jingles to have stuck in your head, particularly if it gives you that reminder to be your freak-flag self.

A *thank you very much for flying your freak flag journal* is simply noting at the end of each day three times where you felt like you were being your authentic self that day. Add more than three if you come up with more. On days where you struggle to write, add three and then delve into the past to remember moments where you felt strong and authentically you. Dig deep; those memories will be there somewhere.

8 Comparison: Growing a spine in the present moment

WHAT WOULD YOU DO if you realised all you had was right now? If you are not held back by past horror stories that are replaying in your mind, then life starts to open up. You lengthen your spine, pull your core in and begin to move in the direction of your dreams.

You can fly your freak flag. Feminist icon and political activist Gloria Steinem writes about a similar concept in her book *My Life on the Road*. The example she gives is a purple motorcycle. The purple motorcycle, a little like Elle Woods signature pink outfits in *Legally Blonde*, has stuck with me as a visual example of a freak flag. The story goes that Steinem came across a group of motorbike riders on the road. She wasn't sure what to make of them and wasn't sure she would connect with them. Steinem admits to making all sorts of assumptions about a particular woman before speaking with her. These assumptions are based on what she thought it meant to be a bikie. However, she started a conversation and found out a little bit more about her and her lifestyle.

Her new-found friend talked about how she had avoided riding in the way that she wanted to for many, many years. She talked about riding in the way she thought she was meant to ride, as part of the bikie gang and on a bike that blended into the pack. It wasn't until she retired that she started to change her life more to her liking. She bought a purple motorcycle, and she began to feel like she was leading the life she wanted. Gloria Steinem considers this, and writes, "... I've come to believe that inside, each of us has a purple motorcycle."

Find your purple motorbike

Your challenge is to find and make the most of your purple motorcycle, or freak flag, before you retire. Your purple motorcycle – or your freak flag – is what is uniquely you. It's what matters most to you, what you want to see more of in the world, and what will define you as a leader.

A freak flag is a feeling. It's the core of self-confidence. It's the feeling you get when you lead the pack on your purple motorcycle. Supremely you; not at the expense of anyone around you, but rather for their benefit: to allow them the freedom to fly their freak flags.

Our freak flag enables us to stand tall. To stand proud. That is a moment-by-moment phenomenon. Your freak flag will have days when it is flying half-mast or comes down for some mending; your challenge is to do the work that has it flying more days than not; more moments than not.

Flying your freak flag occurs only in the present moment; you either hold your core strength in a way that serves you or you go wobbly. If you do a plank exercise each day, your core will get stronger. You will feel your strength develop. But between the planks, you must use your core muscles. Use them to stand tall. You build the muscle for a purpose, not just for the sake of a powerful muscle.

At any given moment, you can check in with yourself. Are you pulling your core in and strengthening your spine while standing tall? Alternatively, are you letting your muscle fall away by not drawing on the strength you have built?

Remember that the best comparison is with yourself. Ask yourself whether you can feel your strong core, or whether you must do more work.

If you work from the present moment, and you fly your freak flag, then you start to work authentically. You become the authentic leader that people want. You also give licence to those around you to be their authentic selves. In the same way as checking your core strength in a moment, at any moment you can consider whether you are authentically you. Over time, you will catch yourself flying your freak flag. It will bring a smile to your face.

What will be different today?

It's not an overnight change. It takes courage and commitment. Because it's all about the present moment – just about this moment, right here and right now. You can be a stronger, more confident person any time. If you challenge yourself to pull that core strength in right now, lengthen your spine. Do something different to what you might have done a moment before. Then, you are already on your way to supreme confidence.

The question is: what will that be for you?

On August 7, 1974, Philippe Petit walked a tightrope between the still-under-construction Twin Towers of the World Trade Centre in New York. Philippe walked for 45 minutes, danced, and even lay down on the wire. He crossed this high wire eight times. He was 411 meters above the ground.

I'm not sure that I could walk a tightrope and stay on it, even if it was a couple of centimetres off the ground. Even for a few steps, I'd be pretty wobbly. Philippe had been confident in his ability to stay in the present moment and complete the task. All he needed to do was take the next step, and the next step, and the next step. It was very much about blocking out everything else, blocking out the 'what if' and blocking out the horror movie. If anything could have made him wobble, it would have been a horror movie preview.

Plan your tightrope walk

Philippe Petit took six years to plan the World Trade Centre walk. Planning and training. It wasn't easy. The training you do to become your more-confident self will, in time, enable you to walk your metaphorical tightrope. However, all training starts with a decision in a moment.

Life is, after all, just a bunch of moments. Moment followed by moment.

Each moment is an opportunity to build on your best. You must make a choice between being stopped in your tracks by imaginative thinking about the past or shifting your focus to this moment and making the most of it. For most of us, that doesn't involve walking a tightrope! It consists of taking small steps that serve us as the leaders.

It might be to do something you have been putting off or avoiding, such as planning a problematic conversation and going through with it. It might be reflecting on what matters most to you so that you can move in that direction with purpose and focus. Choose to do one small action that will make a difference to your sense of self, your sense of confidence.

You are not Philippe Petit, and neither am I. Although, we are all human beings just like Philippe Petit. Human beings can take small steps every day that either build on who they are or detract from who they are.

If you avoid doing the work that will improve your personal best, or if you avoid working on the present moment and avoid building your core strength, then you will not move forward. You risk falling off your tightrope.

There is no box to tick

Remember this is a journey. It's not about attaining perfection. It's humanly impossible to find the present moment and stay in it and never leave it. (That is, arrive at the destination and never leave.) You are human; you get distracted. Your mind works at a speed that can both build and shift metaphorical mountains. So, it's unrealistic to think that you will get to a point where you can tick the box on self-confidence and move onto the next challenge.

Self-confidence is about improving your moment-by-moment experience as a leader. It's about finding yourself in the present moment and standing tall more often as time goes on. It needs a conscious effort from you to be present, to be authentically you and proudly fly your freak flag.

You will be challenged as a leader daily. Some days will be easy. Some days you will feel like throwing it in. The work will feel hard, and your confidence will get knocked. However, the more you do to build your core strength, the easier it will become for you to manage the more difficult days and moments.

If you punch the stomach of someone with a strong core who has flexed their muscles, it will hurt you more than it hurts them. If you hit someone in the stomach who has not been doing the work on core strength, you can do some severe damage.

You have a choice as a leader. You can do the work that will have you feel you are leading the life you were born to live; or, you can wallow in self-doubt. You have a choice. You can challenge your current beliefs, or you can believe them. There is no other choice. It's an unconscious choice you make most of the time, so the "present-moment" work enables you to challenge your thinking and make a more conscious choice around what you choose to believe.

Be the leader we need you to be

We need leaders that show up. We want leaders who are present in the here and now. When did you last hear someone say, "When I talk to that person, I feel as if there's no one else in the room. Nothing matters other than this conversation." Charismatic leaders make us feel heard, feel seen and that we matter. Your ability to lead a team, an organisation, or a country requires you to connect with those you lead. If you don't show up in the present moment, or if you don't focus on that present moment, then you miss the opportunity.

Remember the 'currency in the bank' concept earlier in this book? Congruent actions build up your currency in the bank. Growing a spine is about building up your currency with those you lead. Make those around you feel heard, feel seen, feel that they matter. That requires you to work your "present-moment" muscle.

Most of us crave that feeling of recognition or sense of being seen. The people we lead often look for that from us. The more you show up in the moment, then the more you connect with your people. And, in so doing, you feel more like your true self. You recognise your worth and become a better leader over time.

This point about being truly present is powerful on its own. You could work on being in the present moment, and you'll find that significant changes occur. Some core strength will develop over time. However, if you combine being present with reflecting on the loop that keeps holding you back (which I described in the last chapter), and then you do the work that I cover in the final section (about your future), your leadership starts to come together.

Positive communication with yourself, positive self-comparison in the present moment, and a life-long journey of developing competence add up to a strong self-confidence muscle. Only then will you be able to rely on that muscle on the days where it feels all too hard.

This work is intensely personal. No one else is in your head. No one else can see your horror movie previews. No one else can see your deepest dreams or nightmares. Those around you can challenge you to do the work. They can help you and be your cheerleader, but you must do the work.

You must make a choice; no-one else but just you.

The triple-A approach to self-confident leadership

So, you chose to do the work? Great. Let's make this work a little easier. Think of it as a three-step process: authenticity, acceptance and alignment.

Authenticity

I have covered **authenticity** a couple of times already. It's a word that gets bandied around a lot because it is such an essential element of self-confident leadership. It's at the heart of the freak flag concept.

One of the vital elements found in author Brené Brown's work *The Gifts of Imperfection* is about *cultivating* authenticity. It may sound a little strange, so let me explain.

You can cultivate authenticity by letting go of what people think about you or what you think you are supposed to be. Embrace who you are. Fly your freak flag. I love Brown's use of the word cultivating. It is a reminder that this is a continual process; a journey and not a destination. If you grow plants in a garden, you cultivate. They have a season; they grow, bloom, ripen, fade (or get eaten). Then, you start again. The same is true for authenticity. Moment by moment, you will you feel yourself growing in confidence, just like you are blooming. Some moments you will feel the need to practice self-care, rest and start again.

Cultivating authenticity is about getting clear on who you are and being proud of yourself. Proud of the journey you are on and proud of what makes you unique.

This work is best done as a reflection in quiet time alone. It's when you can explore what's in your heart and what your freak flag looks like. It can also happen in a moment. For example, at this moment right now, are you in harmony with yourself? If the answer is yes, then terrific – your freak flag is flying freely. If the answer is no, ask yourself why. What's holding you back? What can you do right now to shift your thoughts, to shift the comparison you are making with others to a comparison with yourself, and your personal best? Is there one small step you can take to feel you are cultivating authenticity, rather than cutting yourself down?

Acceptance

Acceptance is connected to authenticity because, when you accept who you are, you become authentic. Accept what IS right now – what is in the present. Recognise you are not the perfect leader (because the ideal leader does not exist). Accept that you have arrived at a particular point in your journey.

Start by accepting the things of which you are proud (because that is so much easier). Make a list of everything you are pleased to have achieved. List some of the skills you bring to your role. Get clear on what you offer and be grateful and accepting of those gifts. Embrace who you are.

In the last chapter, I unpacked the negative self-talk. In this chapter, I want you to make the most of favourable comparison. That is about recognising and building up the positive communication that you have with yourself and recognising your worth. Accept your worth, but also accept your flaws.

We are all fallible. We are all flawed. We must celebrate this and not cover it up.

We're not on a journey to perfection. We're on a journey of self-confidence. So, acceptance includes starting to recognise what you must improve. Accept where you are right now but choose to take the path of self-improvement. I'll talk more about self-improvement in chapter nine.

And just so we are clear, acceptance is not the same as resigning or settling. It's about reality checking.

Think about the acceptance that's required to lose weight. If you are carrying more weight than is healthy for you, then you must accept that as a fact. However, if you negatively respond to that fact, then you will struggle to take the necessary action to lose the weight. You will berate yourself and feel so low that you don't want to change. Accept yourself with loving kindness for what IS right now – your current personal best.

Acceptance means looking at the reality of what is and taking the appropriate next step. Don't judge why it is. It just is. You have a choice to improve or stay static. Stay stuck. Acceptance is harder than resignation. Resigning leaves you powerless, but there can be a comfort in that. Acceptance is stronger; bolder. It demands appropriate action. Acceptance of what IS right now does not include approval of what will *always* be. This moment passes, and you move onto the next.

Shift into the driver's seat. Accept what sort of car you are driving and drive it to the best of its capability. You have an opportunity to shift, to make a decision, and move things in a better direction. But, part of that is acknowledging and accepting where you are right now. To be in the driver's seat, you must know where the car is on the road. You must be in the car and not floating above it while looking for a better model.

Alignment

When you decide to change, you had better check that you are changing as you intended. That takes us back to the question of your comparator. Imagine for a moment that you are a supermodel. Imagine you are Kate Moss and you have been on the cover of every fashion magazine. The photo on that magazine looks like an accurate reflection of a human being called Kate Moss.

But is it?

The work it takes for that photo to be created – hours of hair styling and carefully applied make-up, the art and science of good studio lighting, choices on clothes. For one moment, one photograph.

Then it gets 'photoshopped;' that near-perfect image of Kate changed by digital means.

The moment is lost. It's not Kate Moss anymore; it's a computerised version of a photo – her teeth whitened; her cheekbones enhanced. Sometimes limbs are thinned, skin smoothed, and blemishes that the make-up didn't hide removed.

It must be hard being Kate Moss, and being accustomed to seeing photoshopped versions of reality. Acceptance for Kate Moss must be hard work. She has her own "real-looking-yet-non-existent-and-perfect" Kate Moss in front of her on the pages of a magazine.

Consider your imagined prototype perfect leader. Consider how photoshopped your version of them really is, as compared to the reality. It might be a version that was photoshopped by them, or those around them. Or it might be photoshopped by you in the way you blend out their imperfections and areas for development as if they don't exist.

The work you do on acceptance enables you to look at yourself clearly; no make-up or stylish haircut; no fashionable clothes or suit – simply you as you are.

Alignment is where you get creative. It's where you get to think about and create the best version of yourself. (Minus the photoshop. If you photoshop your image of alignment, you slip back into non-acceptance.)

However, alignment is ever so much more important than hair and clothes. So, let's leave the photoshop analogy behind now and focus on how we get clear on alignment.

Alignment is about setting a goal for your next personal best. Get clear on what you must do next, and whether it is in alignment with the goals you have set for yourself. Or, does it take you in a different direction?

It's time for some reflection again. Consider the following in order:

- What's most important to you? (In life, at work, in a team environment... choose your focus.)
- What are you most wanting to achieve? (In this role, this week, this month, or in this life. Again, choose the focus that fits.)

- Are you crystal clear on that for which you are aiming? What does your next personal best looks like?
- If you ask yourself, at any given moment, whether your actions are in alignment with that goal – could you answer the question?
- Are your actions in alignment with that goal right now? (Chances are, the fact that you are doing this reflection will mean that you can answer yes. Then again, consider where you need to shift your activity.)
- Which version of yourself have you accepted as your comparator? Is it the best comparator you can use? Is it a past personal best for you?
- Can you see yourself achieving your identified goal? And if not, go back to step one and start again.
- And finally, what does it look like? How do you feel? Have you felt that way before? Make it as clear as possible in your mind.

Alignment is about being in the present moment and growing your spine, including your strength of purpose. Your spine says: this is who I am, and this is the path I am taking. If I want an aligned spine, or if I want to stand tall and fly my freak flag, then I must be clear on who I am. I must clarify that for which I stand, and what I'm working towards.

Alignment requires some initial reflection, and then it becomes a moment-by-moment question (and answer) activity. It enables you to know whether your actions (at any given moment) serve you, or whether they are taking you down the wrong path.

Alignment is about standing tall; lengthening the spine. Knowing that you are where you are meant to be at this moment.

What's next?

The present moment is the one that matters and the only moment that ever matters. It's this moment; right now. At any moment, you can choose to be authentic. You can decide to fly your freak flag and give licence to those around you to do the same. You can live here and now, in this moment. Or, you can duck back behind the trees and watch the horror movie. It's your choice. The more you show up in the present, then the more you will move forward, rather than stay behind.

You don't want to go to your deathbed thinking, "Oh shit. All that matters is this moment now. I wasted so much time worrying about what might happen and didn't do what I wanted to do. I didn't ride my purple motorcycle." You want to create new memories in each moment, rather than replaying the old ones.

The present moment is a powerful moment. Get ready to feel that power. Feel the centredness of a strong spine. Feel your core strength as your whole being shows up, right here and right now. Now, it's time to create the future; the reality in which you want to step into in the next moment.

What does the next moment look like for you? Is it shining, bright, and exciting? Or, is it dark and foreboding? Your answer will be a clue to whether you are working from the past, the present, or the future.

FOCUSED ACTIONS

Start action with acceptance
Accept what IS right now in the present. Recognise you are not the perfect leader (and neither is that other person you have been idolising). Accept that you have arrived at a particular point in your journey. Recognise yourself in this moment.

Recognise your current personal best
Once you have accepted the present moment, recognise and capture your current personal best. This becomes your helpful comparison as you build on your competence in this area.

Check your alignment
If you ask yourself, at any given moment, whether your actions are in alignment with what matters most to you, then could you answer the question? Which version of yourself have you accepted as your comparator? When did you last pull your core in and stand tall? Reflect on these questions. Take small actions that have you feeling aligned and connected to the real here and now.

9   Competence: Make it a full body experience – let's put it all together

OKAY, SO NOW WHAT YOU ASK? Well, if you have changed your self-communication to be supportive, and you are working on your competence day by day, based on a helpful self- comparison, then what else is left?

Life. It tends to throw us curve balls. So, we need to be prepared. And we need to keep getting up and trying again. And again.

There is a reason why so many change projects in a corporate setting fail. In a 2008 McKinsey study, it was found that only one in three change projects succeeded. Similar findings have been reported in a number of other studies, hence the touted statistic that 70% of change efforts fail.

What do change projects have to do with self-confidence?

They are both about changing what we do as human beings.

Whether you are changing confidence levels, getting someone to go to the gym regularly, or getting a group of people to use a new business process – each is about getting a human being (or a group of human beings) to make a change to the way they currently go about their daily lives. A change to their "default system."

As human beings, we gravitate towards what's comfortable. We gravitate to what we know and what we find easy. We gravitate to our default setting of how we currently do things.

We might be sold on a new fitness program or might see the

logic in a new business process. We might be encouraged to find new ways of comparing ourselves with our personal best, but we need to find ways of holding ourselves accountable to this new insight.

This is about shifting, just a little, from what's in your comfort zone. That's where the growth occurs.

So, what do I do first?

Throughout this book, I've used the body as a metaphor. I've talked about straightening your spine and building strength in your core. Pulling it all together and building your competence in self-confidence is a little like working on your *overall* fitness – and I mean overall: muscle strength, flexibility and cardiovascular fitness. Yep, it's a little like creating your own fitness plan.

When you work a muscle, you strengthen that muscle. If you don't work that muscle, then the muscle just fades away. In the same way, manager competence can either be built up over time or it can start to fade. The same is true for competence in self-confidence.

When we sign up for a new fitness regime, unless we are on a reality TV show, we don't sign up for it and take a break from life and our other responsibilities. We add it into our lives. We decide that we are going to leave work earlier and go for a walk. We decide that we are going to that yoga class at lunchtime, or that spin class before work. We fit it in. We add it to our calendar and our daily regime because we can see that it will make a difference in our ability to meet the other demands of our lives.

Building self-confidence is the same. We need to find ways to include the building of confidence into our every day. There is no magic pill; and, reading this book alone will not be enough. You need to do the work regularly. You need to be aware of the tools available to you that will have you shift the self-doubt, but you also need to use them.

Competency and comparison

Let's use the metaphor of fitness again while honing in on the building of muscle to understand competency's relationship with comparison.

All that matters is how strong your muscle is today, and what you can do to make it stronger. *Today*. If I build my muscles in a gym, I might get distracted from time to time by those around me. I might slip into comparison with others, thinking: 'Urgh, I will always suck. I will never have big enough or strong enough muscles.'

However, if I come back to this moment, I have a choice. I can lift a weight and build my muscle right now. Or, I can fall into the negative comparison trap and not do the work. Of critical importance here is that comparison with self requires us to lift the next weight level that's right for us. We add weights or repetitions based on our current personal best, not based on the weight lifter next to us.

When it comes to building competence, including competence in self-confidence, you must be clear that your comparison is with yourself. No one else.

Competency and communication

When you recognise competency as a journey and not a destination, you can be respectful and kind to yourself about where you find yourself today. You accept what is and act accordingly. You consider alignment with where you want to go, and you then do the work. You support yourself with positive reinforcement as you lift the weight.

When you acknowledge the journey you are on, you enable yourself to enjoy learning something new every day in the area of leadership. If you think about competence-building in this way – that it is something you are going to do each day, then you will find something new to learn each day and it becomes less daunting. It enables you to move to a growth mindset about your development as a leader, including the development of your self-confidence. It's a small step each day to improve the way you work and how you function in your role. It's that next repetition, or weight level, to build the muscle.

Competence-building then becomes easier because it is about the small step you take today. Don't worry about what you might be in three months' time or three years' time, but rather what you are doing *today*. You don't build muscles by saying, "In three years' time, I'm going to be able to lift 30 kilograms," and then do nothing about it. Rather, you build muscles each day by stretching yourself that little bit further and lifting a heavier weight. It becomes doable, and it is a less arduous task when it is broken down into the day-by-day steps.

When you start to work on competence in a step-by-step and day-by-day way, you gain momentum. Confidence comes in part from this momentum, feeling as if you know more today than you did yesterday or last week. All you must do is put one foot in front of the other each day. Start that journey rather than standing still.

Strengths, Stretches and Supporters

When it comes to competence in self-confidence, and for that matter competence as a leader, there are three areas you need to consider: strengths, stretches and supporters.

Strengths

The quickest way to improve, and the most satisfying, is to *build* on and *balance* your strengths. Consider for a moment: if you have worked with a personal trainer in a gym, have they ever spoken about 'removing your weakness'? No! They talk about building strength. They also talk about not overusing muscles and the importance of rest days. This is great advice for leaders too. So, when it comes to getting the most out of your strengths, think build and balance.

Self-confidence is about knowing what is innately *you* and letting it shine through (aka fly your freak flag). It's about looking at and acknowledging your strengths (*your* muscles) – comparison with *your* personal best. And, it's not trying to conform to a non-existent perfect leader.

So, how do you identify your current strengths?

VIA Survey of Character Strengths

One of the best tools that I've come across when it comes to strengths is the VIA Survey of Character Strengths. It was developed by positive psychology guru, Martin E. P. Seligman.

www.authentichappiness.sas.upenn.edu/testcenter

To access the results, you will need to log in and answer a few questions. Your answers are part of Seligman's ongoing research into authentic happiness. However, the 15-minute survey produces a report that's great to read and will give you a sense of what is uniquely you. The survey identifies your key strengths and reveals what is vital to your happiness.

As with your key values, the survey identifies what qualities you gravitate towards and what is critical to feeling happy in the way that you work. These are the things that you need to make part of your every day. Part of the way you work. This is about amplifying or making the most of your strengths, rather than putting them aside to work on your "weaknesses." This is about finding and riding your purple motorcycle.

You are a legend

One of the tools that helps with your sense of internal narrative and sense of personal strength is the creation of a Legend's Folder. This was a concept that thought leader and co-founder of the Thought Leader's Business School, Peter Cook, came up with to help maintain mojo levels. He creates a physical folder, called the Legend's Folder, which he reads once a month. It's a combination of emails, letters, or anything that somebody has sent him which says, "You're amazing at this." Or, "Thank you so much for helping me." Or, "I think you're a wonderful person for these reasons; you are a legend." The Legend's Folder is all about you and your strengths; reminders that you've had an amazing impact on others. It's an important and helpful way of giving yourself a boost once a month.

Cook recommends you diarise reading your Legend's Folder every month. If you haven't kept these emails or these letters, then start today. Look out for them and build your folder as you go. And in the meantime, sit down and write what you have achieved in your life thus far that makes you proud. That's the first page of your legend's folder. You can keep adding to it throughout your career.

Competency audit

Now, pull out your position description that you reviewed in Chapter Three – or find your position description now. If you don't have one, search your role on the internet and find an equivalent position description. From your position description, make a neat list of skills you need to be successful in your role.

The list might look something like this (or quite different; remember it's specific to your role):

- Preparing and maintaining budgets and working within an approved budget;
- Setting strategic direction for the team;
- Managing people challenges, engaging and developing my team;
- Developing and maintaining strong stakeholder relationships with key people and organisations;
- Preparing board papers;
- Briefing the CEO on key areas of risk within my portfolio and area of expertise; and,
- Overseeing a pipeline of work, and delivery of key projects through my leadership of the team.

Now, give yourself a score out of 10 for each of the areas you have identified.

We all judge ourselves constantly. This is your opportunity to judge yourself in a constructive way. Review the scores you gave yourself. Some may be eight, nine or 10. They are the areas where you go, "Tick. These are my strengths. I need to keep working them, but if I only work on these, then that's not going to help me."

Let this process remind you of your strengths; they will likely be the reasons why you got the job. However, as this is about building competence, we need to go a step further.

Look at the other end of the spectrum from zero to three. If you have areas that fall into this category, then look for someone you know and trust. Find someone who is highly competent in that area. Work with them and *learn* from working with them, but don't worry too much about trying to build strength in this area yet.

Now, identify the middle range from four to seven. These are the areas in which you need to build some strength so that you can balance out the list. These are your growth edge areas of competence.

They are the skills that you need to focus on next. They will be skills where you have a working knowledge of what needs to be done, but you do not feel skilled or competent in this area yet.

Now, prioritise them. What will you work on first? What is the first next step to build your competence in that area? Choose the areas that involve the least effort and deliver the biggest impact. As you grow in competence in these areas, your self-confidence will in turn feel a significant boost.

Don't go it alone

Do the work yourself first. Trust the data and understand your own strengths. But, don't go it alone. Road test the outcomes with your supporters (see below). For example, if you do the position description exercise and you don't have anything that is a 10 out of

10, road test that with a supporter who believes you are capable of doing the role you're in. They may have a different view.

Stretches

If you work a muscle to build its strength, you must also stretch it regularly so that the muscle stays healthy and flexible. The same is true for competence building and the building of self-confidence. Stretching must be your new favourite thing: stretching yourself a little bit further than you did yesterday.

Use your strengths to stretch into your growth areas

Starting with strengths helps quell negative inner narratives. If you are thinking, "I suck at maths, or I suck at presentations, or I suck at board reports" – or whatever you are worried about, then you must find a replacement narrative.

For example, you might need to replace a negative narrative of "I have no idea when it comes to profit and loss statements". A positive replacement narrative may be, "I am great at making connections with people. I'm going to make a connection with a key person in the finance team. Once the connection is made, I will ask them about how the profit and loss statements work. In the meantime, because I love reading, I will read a couple of articles about profit and loss statements."

Growth edges are about building on the positive; building from strength. Understanding what to stretch, and then taking that next step; leaning-in to the stretch with confidence because you know it's going to help build your competence.

Too many people try to do the metaphorical "splits" in a day when it comes to competence building. Trying to do this can result in significant damage. If one of your areas for growth is presentations, maybe the next step is to talk to a great presenter about how they prepare and what they do. Your next step will NOT be signing up to make a 30-minute presentation at the executive meeting next week, which might have you 'strain a muscle' and do damage that you will then have to repair. That presentation will come but take the small steps that will get you there. Ask for help along the way.

Work out the stretch that will push you just enough to grow and to learn. One good way is to create a to-do list of those small steps. Make sure that you do one step each day, or at least each week, to build your competence in this area.

If you stretch yourself a little each day, you will see a two-fold result: your self-confidence increases and your competence increases too. You double the result. You benefit personally, and those around you will see your competence and your confidence growing.

As with identifying strengths, you must do the work initially yourself. But again, it's important to test this out with trusted advisors – your supporters. That trusted advisor will be the one that says, "No. Don't sign up for that 30-minute presentation next week. Instead, let's chat about what your next step might be. Perhaps do a five-minute presentation in two weeks' time. Let's work on how you can nail it." That, in turn, improves your confidence and competence.

Supporters

Supporters are essential to your success. All great leaders have supporters around them and use them wisely. These are the people you turn to for guidance and advice. Pick them carefully. They are like personal trainers; they want the best for you and are more experienced than you in a particular area. They will challenge you fairly, appropriately and help you grow.

As you will see from the examples below, they may be people known to you, and people with whom you spend time. Or, they may be people you watch from afar.

My MOMs – meeting of the minds – group

I'm lucky to come from a large family. I have a brother and a sister who think and work in a similar way to me. A few years ago, we created a little group called the MOMs Group. MOM stands for Meeting of the Minds. The three of us meet regularly, or we message or call each other regularly. We understand and value each other. We acknowledge and talk about how lucky we feel to have the support of the group. We challenge each other appropriately when we feel that one of us needs to be challenged. We celebrate our wins together as well.

That support network is vital to the way I have worked in the last few years. Each of us talks about how our MOMs Group helped us grow. Remember, this chapter is about competence. You don't grow in competence if you are not challenging yourself and being appropriately challenged by your supporters.

Supporters are however different to just a friend. I'll use a movie analogy here again. In the movie *He's Just Not That into You*, the central character Gigi is a single woman who reads too much in to her dates and convinces herself they are romantically interested in her. Then, she frets when they don't call.

There is an exchange at the start where her friends tell her, "No, he'll call. He's going to call. It's not you; it's him. Maybe he's held up; maybe he's lost your number." They give her every excuse under the sun for why her date didn't call. The same can be true with friends who say, "No, you're doing great. You'll be fine." Ultimately, that's not enough and you need to be challenged. The supporter is the one who says, "You're doing a great job, and you've got a whole lot of value that you can give here. This is where you must focus your energy to do a better job, and to reach that next level that I know you want to."

In the movie *He's Just Not That into You*, the supporter might have said, "Maybe you need to think about why it's so important to you that he calls. Perhaps the call itself is not the right focus. Let's go for a walk and talk about all the things that are working really well for you right now, and what your next goal is that is within your control."

When I decided to leave the corporate world and start a consulting business, it was my MOMs Group that took me through my paces for the decision I had come to (my why). They questioned the planning I had done (the how) and held me to account on the when. I also had a financial planner who asked me the right questions and helped the planning piece come together. These supporters are critical, so seek them out. If you are not lucky enough to be the youngest of nine siblings, then find your next best alternative. Find the people that you need in your corner to challenge you in a highly supportive way.

Find a mentor or three

A mentor is a person that helps you with a particular growth edge. A mentor can be a mentor for a moment, they can be a mentor for a lifetime, and everything in between. There is a short video on LinkedIn by Suzy Welch, an American author, television commentator, business journalist, and public speaker who is married to Jack Welch – the former chair and CEO of global company, General Electric.

Suzy Welch says anyone can be a mentor. When she was a young reporter, she thought of a fellow reporter as the epitome of the super leader. This was the person she thought could do no wrong. She read everything that they wrote. She wanted to understand and learn from them. Much later on in life, they became good friends. She said it was following them, reading them, and understanding what they did that made the biggest difference in her career. That was her example of how you can find a mentor.

Remember not to compare yourself to them. Go back to your personal best and find the next step you can take that pushes you to their direction.

One of my favourite books most recently is Kristen Hadeed's: *Permission to Screw Up: How I learned to Lead by Doing (Almost) Everything Wrong.* Kristen Hadeed set up a business called "Student Maid." It was a cleaning service in the United States that tapped into two needs: students who wanted casual work and student accommodation that needed to be cleaned. Hadeed saw a business need and the business took off quickly. She learned on the run and the narrative in her book highlights just how human she is as a leader.

Hadeed has done exceptionally well, both financially and as a leader. But, she learnt by doing things wrong. She recognised her errors and found solutions to fix them. She grew in competence and confidence. I just love her honesty and openness about how tough it was. She is a supporter.

It's important to seek out successful people who are open about their own fragility as human beings, and their own growth edges. Read their books or talk to them. The more you find out about them, the more you recognise that we are all on a journey. And, the better you are able to support everybody else around you.

What's next?
Competence building is simply a journey of learning new skills and building up your 'competence muscles.' Competence building is critical to your continued success. Build on your personal strengths, focus on small, regular stretches, and do it all alongside your supporters.

Our ability to learn and improve is infinite. Muscles diminish quickly with lack of use compared with muscles that build from everyday use. The beauty of competence building is you feel better each day.

I'm an avid reader. I learn something new with each book I read, usually many things. I think of competence in the same way: it's just learning something new. Every day I learn something new, I am a better leader and a better person, as well as a more competent person and a more confident leader.

Now it's up to you. You can put this book back on the shelf or you can take action today.

What's your next step? Is it towards a brighter and more confident future or back in the doubt-filled past?

FOCUSED ACTIONS

Who are your supporters
Find a mentor or three! A mentor is a person who helps you with a particular growth edge. A mentor can be your mentor for a moment, a lifetime, and everything in between. Supporters are essential to your success. All great leaders have supporters and relate to them wisely. Remember, they understand and value you. They will challenge you appropriately, fairly and with love and respect. They will celebrate your wins with you.

Get to know those you admire
Read what they have written, listen to their podcasts, watch their videos, or attend an event. Understand what they did that made the biggest difference in their career or their life.

But remember: don't compare yourself to them! Go back to your personal best, a strong spine, a strong core and the present moment. From there, you can fairly and accurately assess what action you can take in the right direction. Consider what you can learn from them and do differently.

You are a legend
Create a "Legends folder" that you can regularly re-read and enjoy. This folder is full of the emails, letters and comments people make about you that build your confidence. Remember, this folder is all about you. It is about your strengths and the positive impact you have on others. It becomes a useful tool, giving you a boost as you add to it and read it. Make time to do this once a month.

Create a MOMs Group
MOM means Meeting of the Minds group. Build one. Find like-minded leaders who want to work on confidence, or competence in a particular area together. Write the ground rules for the group. Understand and value each other. Challenge each other appropriately and fairly. Assist each other to become stronger and more confident. Build each other up. And lastly, celebrate each little win!

What now?

SO, WE KNOW NOW THAT CONFIDENCE comes from a combination of consistent positive self-communication, comparison for good (not ill) and leaning-in to the building of competence along the journey of leadership.

These are all manageable actions. Small bites of the big elephant of confidence.

It all starts with a single step

Based on my years of work with executives and other leaders, in my different roles as a lawyer, general manager, business owner and coach, I know that things will change if you take these steps. I've seen it happen many times and it is a beautiful thing to see.

I've seen it happen the other way too. If you don't take action or if you don't counter the internal narrative, then you can end up running yourself off the rails.

The work involved with communication, comparison, and competence is lifelong work. There is no ultimate destination or nirvana when it comes to confidence or leadership.

Life will throw you curveballs, so the more you're familiar with your self-doubt, unhelpful comparisons, and relationship with learning, the better you will manage the curveballs with grace. One day, if not today, you'll have people looking at you thinking you are the prototype, non-existent perfect leader.

We need to consciously work on these areas. We need to take small steps every day. These steps are a little bit scary. They really put us out there and stretch us appropriately. We need to be proud of ourselves for what we've achieved already and look forward rather than backwards to a future that is magnificent. But, don't miss this moment right now and don't miss the opportunity for action that will take you forward.

Overcome the (inevitable) obstacles

You will fall down. You will get feedback you don't like. You will feel like you're failing. You will have bad days. This is life. What matters is what you tell yourself on those days. Do you say, "Urgh, I suck." Or, do you say: "Okay, that wasn't pleasant. What now"? Or, in the words of my favourite fictional U.S. president, Josiah (Jed) Bartlet from The West Wing, "What's next?" Stay in action. Move on. Don't get stuck in the repeated horror movie preview.

Accept the invitation

Sometimes you need to talk to someone who has been there and knows the pathway. Make sure you seek out the people that will help you on your journey. This may be an executive coach, or it may be a mentor or trusted friend. This is the work I love. I love seeing leaders grow in this way. I love seeing them flying their freak flag with flourish.

Proudly fly your Freak Flag

The self-confident leaders who understand and work on communication, comparison, and competence are what makes the world a better place. In small, conversational ways and in large-statement ways. These are the leaders who understand their fragility as humans and celebrate what makes them unique. They fly their freak flag. They give licence to those around them to do the same.

In 1994, President Nelson Mandela, in making his inaugural speech, quoted Marianne Williamson:

"Our deepest fear is not that we are inadequate. Our deepest fear is that we are powerful beyond measure. It is our light, not our darkness, that most frightens us. We ask ourselves: Who am I to be brilliant, gorgeous, talented, fabulous? Actually, who are you not to be? ... as we let our own light shine, we unconsciously give other people permission to do the same. As we're liberated from our own fear, our presence automatically liberates others."

It's a quote that struck a chord with me at the time and it still does today. It's my hope that everyone reading this book will feel that the time has come to let their light shine brightly and proudly.

Gratitude to those who made this book possible

A BOOK ABOUT CONFIDENCE IS NOT AN EASY ONE TO COMPOSE. At times, it was exceedingly difficult to maintain confidence in the editing process. The process has been one in which I was forced to take my own medicine. I have often had to check my internal narrative and reframe my "I Suck at editing" stories. I have had to abstain from comparing myself to the "seemingly perfect" Amy Cuddy and Dr. Brené Brown. I have had to lean into the competency-building exercise of getting my ideas into written form. On this final point, I was sure to surround myself with people who could fill the gaps in my areas of competency when it comes to book writing. And, I could not have done this without them.

The first person on my team was Kath Walters. I met Kath, serendipitously, a number of years ago when we commenced a course together. I have a theory that, when you meet someone who is going to play a meaningful part in your life, your soul somehow marks the introduction subconsciously. I met a number of people the day on which I met Kath – upwards of around 30 people. I didn't know why at the time, but meeting Kath was memorable. I know why now. This book would not have come into being if it were not for Kath's guidance, support and expertise. Kath has been there from the first conversation. And, she is still here today as I complete the final touches on the manuscript. I will be forever grateful to Kath for her expertise, her guidance and support, her ability to keep me accountable and her own experience of my content – she even watched Legally Blonde!

The next person I have to thank is one of my team members, Madeleine Armstrong. By the time this book is published, Maddy will have spread her wings and taken up her dream role as an employment and safety lawyer – a move I am so proud to see her make. I also remember the first time I met Maddy. An exceptionally talented young woman who I have had the pleasure of working with now for twelve months. Maddy has read this manuscript in many guises, encouraged me, and edited key aspects for me as well – particularly on days when I was very stuck in the "I suck at editing" story! Maddy gave me confidence that my work was needed. I will fondly remember sitting next to her a few times as she laughed out loud, reading chapters for the first time. I will also remember how she relayed to me that she had put aspects of it into practice while preparing for an important interview. How lucky I feel to have been introduced to Maddy. Which leads me to Steve Clifford.

Steve Clifford is the reason why I became a lawyer. I had the amazing good fortune of meeting Steve through a clerkship in Singapore when I was partway through my law degree. Steve was my guiding light – through his example, I could see that I could be a lawyer and still have a soul. Relevant to the context of this book, Steve had confidence in me long before I had the same level of confidence in myself. The gift of having confidence in someone else before they can see it themselves is powerful. I have a very clear memory from my first week of working with Steve while I was still a law student. He pointed to a magazine cover featuring Christine Lagarde, who is now the head of the International Monetary Fund. But, at the time, she was the first female chair of International Law Firm Baker & McKenzie. Steve remarked, conversationally but with confidence, "That could be you one day." Of course, my immediate internal reaction was one of: "You've got to be kidding me." And yet, at the same time, the seed was planted. I thought to myself: "What can he see in me that I am not seeing myself?" It planted a seed deep enough that this memory is still crystal-clear today. One moment in time, where someone saw something in me. As leaders, our challenge is to put our heads up often enough to provide this sort of gift to those around us who need encouragement – who need their internal narrative challenged.

We need to surround ourselves with people who can – and will – challenge our internal narrative as required. Who back us and build us up when we need it the most. To that end, I could write another book on the people who have been there for me and provided the important confidence boost as required along the way. All the same, I will limit myself to three core groups of people who have been particularly important into bringing this book into being.

The Corvus Group Australia team (which of course includes Maddy) have been there from the start. Asking questions on progress, reading early drafts and providing encouragement at every turn. Thank you in particular to my business partner, Martin Richardson, for his support of this work from the very start.

Then, there is the Meeting of the Minds (MOMs) group. This is a small group of three; the three youngest children of my parents. My brother Andy, my sister Gen and me. This group challenges me and attempts to keep me accountable. Further, it provides me with a significant sense of both support and strength.

And finally, but most importantly, there are the three loves of my life: my husband Tim, my daughter Eleanor and my mum Brenda, all of to whom I dedicate this book. I would not be who I am today if it were not for their continual good influence on me, love for me, and confidence in me.

Index